THE BOOK OF MARA

Mara, sorella: perdonami
Maggio del 1919

Mara, sister: forgive me
May 1919

The Book of Mara

BY
ADA NEGRI

TRANSLATED BY
MARIA A. COSTANTINI

ITALICA PRESS
NEW YORK
2011

Copyright © 2011 by Maria A. Costantini

ITALICA PRESS, INC.
595 Main Street, Suite 605
New York, New York 10044

All rights reserved. No part of this publication may be reproduced, stored in a retrieval system, or transmitted, in any form or by any means, electronic, mechanical, photocopying, recording, or otherwise, without prior permission of Italica Press. For permission to reproduce selected portions for courses, please contact the Press at inquiries@italicapress.com.

Library of Congress Cataloging-in-Publication Data
Negri, Ada, 1870–1945.
[Libro di Mara. English & Italian]
The book of Mara / by Ada Negri ; translated by Maria A. Costantini.
  p. cm.
English and Italian.
Includes bibliographical references and index.
Summary: "The first English translation of Ada Negri's 1919 volume of poetry "Il libro di Mara," appearing as a dual-language, facing Italian-English edition, with introduction, bibliography and first-line index. From the highpoint of her career, this work examines the spiritual nature of love, loss and redemption"--Provided by publisher.
  ISBN 978-1-59910-206-1 (hardcover : alk. paper) --
  ISBN 978-1-59910-171-2 (pbk. : alk. paper) --
  ISBN 978-1-59910-195-8 (ebk.)
  I. Costantini, Maria A., 1944- II. Title.
  PQ4831.E4L513 2010
  851'.912--dc22

2010041537

For a Complete List of
Italica Poetry in Translation
Visit our Web Site at
www.ItalicaPress.com

About the Translator

Maria Anna Recchia Costantini was born in the town of Casalvieri, near Rome, Italy, and came to the United States at age twelve. Her work in poetry and prose has the flavor of her Italian heritage and her immigrant experience. It has appeared in literary magazines and anthologies in print and online, and has won prizes and honors in contests by the National Federation of Poetry Societies, the Michigan Poetry Society, William Allen Creative Nonfiction, and Springfed Arts/Metro Detroit Writers. She is affiliated with Springfed Arts/Metro Detroit Writers, the Michigan Poetry Society, and the Dante Alighieri Society.

In late 2006, Costantini began to translate the poetry of Ada Negri, including the Italica Press editions of her translations of *Il Libro di Mara (The Book of Mara)* and *I Canti dell'Isola (Songs of the Island)*. She is currently working on the translation of *Maternità (Motherhood)*, Negri's third book of poetry (1904), as well as two personal projects: a collection of poems and a memoir. Formerly, Maria Costantini worked for twenty-eight years as a Bilingual/English-as-a-Second-Language teacher and chairperson in the Utica Community Schools. She has two grown children and resides in Rochester, Michigan, with her husband Franco.

To the dear memory of my sister-in-law,
Angela Costantini DiMartino

Dopo sì lungo soffrire, 'pace' implora
  il sereno pallor della luna:
pace al cuore ancora vivente, pace al cuore
  che non batte più.

After long suffering, 'peace' entreats
  the serene pallor of the moon:
peace to the heart still living, peace
  to the heart that beats no more.

Quies,
by Ada Negri

Contents

Introduction	IX
Translator's Notes	XIX
Bibliography	XXI
The Book of Mara	1
Il sole e l'ombra	2
The Sun and the Shadow	3
Il Ricordo	4
Remembrance	5
La Crocifissa	8
Crucified	9
Apparizione	10
Apparition	11
Sinfonia azzurra	12
Blue Symphony	13
Quel giorno	14
That Day	15
Notturno nuziale	16
Wedding Nocturne	17
Il risveglio	18
The Awakening	19
Trasumanazione	20
Transhumanation	21
Lettere	22
Letters	23
Il silenzio	24
The Silence	25
O tardi venuto	26
O Latecomer	27
Il figlio	28
The Son	29
Accettazione	30
Acceptance	31
Ascensione	32
Ascension	33
Il vuoto	34
The Void	35
La follia	36
Folly	37
Grido	38
Cry	39
Il muro	40
The Wall	41

Incantesimo	42
Enchantment	43
Il costruttore	44
The Builder	45
Anniversario	46
Anniversary	47
(I sogni) La mano	48
(Dreams) The Hand	49
(I sogni) Lo sguardo	50
(Dreams) The Look	51
(I sogni) Dialogo	52
(Dreams) Dialogue	53
La terra	54
The Earth	55
La lampada d'oro	56
The Golden Lamp	57
Rendimento di grazie	58
Giving Thanks	59
Il colloquio	60
The Conversation	61
Quies	62
Quies	63
Il passante	64
The Passer-By	65
La rinunzia	66
Renunciation	67
Senza addio	68
Without Goodbye	69
Nei giardini del silenzio	70
In the Gardens of Silence	71
Via della Passione	72
Way of the Passion	73
Ode canicolare	74
Summer Ode	75
Notturno della luna	80
Nocturne	81
Pace	82
Peace	83
Voto	84
Vow	85
Domani	86
Tomorrow	87
First Line Index	89

Introduction

A book of poems titled *On the Face of the Waters*[1] by Grace L. Slocum, poet and daughter of the American Revolution, includes a poem titled "Ada Negri":

> Child of the burning South, thou full throated songster,
> Making all hearts ache with thy lyric rapture,
> Pouring forth all thy soul's impassioned longings
> In strains melodious;
>
> As some prisoned bird beats its bars in anguish,
> So thy fettered soul pants and sighs for freedom,
> Fain to stretch its wings in the empyrean,
> Soaring and singing.
>
> Thine the strenuous voice caught afar from Dante;
> Thine the lyric grace and the fire of Sappho;
> And thou too, should'st be crowned with violets,
> O thou sweet singer!
>
> Heart and soul aflame with a noble passion,
> Singing through thy tears, thou hast 'roused a Nation;
> At thy feet they bow, proud to do thee homage,
> O Ada Negri!

It's interesting to note that an American poet wrote an ode to a poet whose work she had probably read in translation, since, by 1898, Boston translator Adelheid Maria von Blomberg had translated Ada Negri's debut collection of poems, *Fatalità* (*Fate*, 1892). To American readers, this volume defined Negri as a poet of democracy,[2] whose poetry *stirs the blood to revolt against oppression and incite to riot and arson*. To readers abroad, regardless of future publications, Negri would always be known as the turn-of-the century

---

1. Boston: Gorham Press, 1911.
2. The Academy 59 (1900).

"social poet," whose voice cried out on behalf of the masses, whose work was meant to effect change. In rough lyrics, they sang of things no one had yet dared express in poetry: the long miseries of unemployment, the mutilated hands of factory women, the workman, broken by his work, the vagabond who never knew a home. They decried the fog-bound industrial centers of Northern Italy, their industrial plants, their desolate workers' districts, the humble interiors of people leading repressed, hopeless lives.

Fatalità appeared in a period of great social unrest, characterized by strikes, by demonstrations violently suppressed, and by the women's emancipation movement. That was also the age of Parnassian taste in literature; by contrast, Negri's descriptions, impassioned, vigorous, and straightforward, bore the unmistakable ring of authenticity that only personal experience can give. Negri knew these things first hand. Her voice was new, sincere, owing little to poetic tradition. Consider a stanza from *Senza nome*, (*Nameless*), the second poem in *Fatalità*:

Senza nome

Io non ho nome,— Io son la rozza figlia
  dell'umida stamberga;
plebe triste e dannata è mia famiglia,
ma un'indomita fiamma in me s'alberga.

Nameless

I have no name—I am the ill-bred daughter
  of a damp hovel;
people sad and damned are my family,
yet inside me dwells an indomitable flame.

Ada Negri, affectionately known as Dinin, is the first Italian writer to emerge from a working class family. Born on February 3rd, 1870, in the town of Lodi, near Milan, she grew up in poverty. Her father, Giuseppe, who worked as cabbie, died when she was one year old. Her mother, Vittoria Cornalba, worked as a weaver in a factory. Negri spent her childhood in the porter's lodge of the Cingia-Barni palace, where her grandmother Peppina Panni was custodian, and spent her days observing the comings and goings of the palace.

But, thanks to her mother's sacrifices, she attended Lodi's Normal School for Girls and earned an elementary teacher's diploma. At eighteen, she took a position as schoolteacher in the village of Motta Visconti, on the Ticino, near Pavia. There, she lived in a miserable house; to reach her room, she had to cross a wide, muddy courtyard onto which the stables opened and where geese were splashing, and then climb two steep flights of worn brick steps. Her window-panes were not of glass, but of paper, and the box that contained her books served her as a divan.

In her introduction to von Blomberg's translation of *Fatalità*, Italian author Sofia Bisi Albini, points out that at the time Negri wrote those poems, she had never seen the sea, nor did she know the mountains, nor even the hills and lakes; nor had she seen a large city until the summer of 1892, when she stayed in Milan for two days with friends.

Many of the poems in *Fatalità* had been previously published in the evening paper of Milan, *Il Corriere della Sera*, as well as *Illustrazione Popolare*. In 1894, Negri was awarded the honorary stipend of the Milli Prize, the sum of 1700 lire a year for the term of ten years. She was also called to teach literature at the Normal School Gaetana Agnese in Milan. Two years later, she published a second volume of poetry, titled *Tempeste (Tempests),* still in the vein of social revolt. With poems such as *Fire in the Mine, Strike, Unemployed,* and *End of the Strike,* the poet again spoke to her country with the voice of the oppressed, working classes, and told of their everyday feelings, aspirations and sufferings. Due to its Socialist theme, this phase of Negri's poetry is known as the "red phase." She was la *vergine rossa*, the red maiden. She was the proletarian Sappho.

After the publication of *Tempeste*, Ada Negri made the following confession: "There is something of greatness, of the absolute, that is fermenting here in my head; maybe from it will come the great word." She believed she would reach the ability to capture the absolute word, to conquer the divine song. She also believed that, even if she were to disappear after *Fatalità* and *Tempeste*, her name would still become legend. She said that her art was tied to the experiences of her life in an indissoluble way and her poetry, written with the fever of blood, gushed forth ready, defined in its ultimate form, with its rough rhythm and rough design.

But, after she married Giovanni Garlanda, a rich manufacturer, in 1896, her readers questioned her sincerity. Some called her an "apostate," who, complacent in her affluence, had turned away from social injustice. Without having met her, Giovanni Garlanda had fallen in love with Ada Negri just by reading her first two books of poetry. Without knowing anything of her life, he wrote to her, asking her to marry him. She accepted and they married one month later. In two years, they had their first child Bianca, and Negri fell ill with anemia. She then gave birth to their second child Vittoria, who died at one month of age. Negri slowly recovered and wrote her third volume, *Maternità (Motherhood,* 1904), wherein the poet entered the second phase of her poetry. Her verses became more introspective, more intimate. They spoke of the joys and sorrows of motherhood, the position of her fellow-women, and the limitations and injustice under which they labored.

Negri felt trapped in her marriage and she left it in 1913, the year in which daughter Bianca went to study in Zurich, Switzerland, and Negri went with her. There she remained until the beginning of World War I. In this period, she wrote *Esilio* (Exile), *Le solitarie* (The solitary ones), and *Orazioni* (Orations). As the war broke out, she returned to Italy, where she volunteered her help in hospitals. She had a tormented relationship with a man whose life was cut short by premature death, an experience she describes in *Il libro di Mara*. These poems were written with unusual frankness, especially in view of the Italian society of the time, strongly Catholic and conservative. In the same year, her mother Vittoria died.

The book's dedication, *Mara, sorella: perdonami,* (Mara, sister: forgive me) is enigmatic, since Ada Negri did not have a sister, but only a brother who died young. The name Mara, of Hebrew origin, means bitter, unhappy. In reference to the Book of Ruth, in the Old Testament, Naomi, wife of Elimelech and mother-in-law of Ruth, took on the name Mara after the death of her husband and her two sons. She said: *Don't call me Naomi, but rather Mara because God has made my life bitter. I left full, but I'm coming back empty. God has brought misfortune on me. (1:20-21)*

Ada Negri writes *The Book of Mara* primarily in the second person (*tu ed il tuo uomo*/ your and your man), addressing herself as Mara, her alter ego. The book traces Mara's journey of love and death, joy and suffering, humbled passion and mutilated flesh, renunciation and acceptance. The verses transmute as they evolve: love in death, joy in suffering, *vicinissimi, lontanissimi*/ so very near, so very far, (*Incantesimo*/ /Enchantment). The flesh shivers in:

Notturno nuziale

*Quando tu venisti, una notte, verso il suo
   letto, al buio,
e le dicesti piano, già sopra di lei: Non ti
   vedo, ti sento.
E la ghermisti con artiglio d'aquila, e tutta
   la costringesti nella tua forza,
riplasmandola in te con tal furore ch'ella
   perdette il senso di esistere.*

Wedding Nocturne

When you came, one night, to her bed,
   in the dark

and told her softly, already upon her: :I don't
see you, I feel you."
And you gripped her with the claw of an eagle,
and compelled all of her with your strength,
re-molding her to you with such fury that she lost
her sense of existence.

Here, love is vigorous, full, and joyous. It later turns to weeping, pleading, in:

Grido

Torna una volta, col grande tuo corpo in ànsito
in vampa sul mio prostrato pallore.
Afferrami come facevi quand'io non ero che amore
tremante dinanzi al tuo amore.

Cry

Come back just one time, with your great body
panting on fire over mine, prostrate and pale.
Grab me as you did when I was but
a trembling love before your love.

Wishing to go beyond the physical boundaries of love in *Trasumanazione* (Transhumanation), Mara wants to join her lover on the pyre of death, so he will belong to no one else, not even death.

Ascesa anch'ella al tuo rogo di morte, per
essere assolta e purificata,
per riaverti dal fuoco, dall'aria, dagli astri, da
ogni bellezza creata.

She too ascended to your funeral pyre, to be
forgiven and purified,
to reclaim you from the fire, from the air, from
the stars, from every beauty created.

In the last three poems of the book, *Pace* (Peace), *Voto* (Vow), and *Domani* (Tomorrow), Mara asks for peace and absolution, reconciliation and hope:

> *Per tutti I pianti ch'io piansi, grazia dei martiri,*
> *   senso di pace, discendi in me:*
> *spoglia ormai d'ogni bene del mondo, placata*
> *   e in ginocchio ti ricevo dal cielo.*

For all the tears I cried, grace of the martyrs,
    feeling of peace, descend upon me:
by now stripped of every good of the world,
    calmed, and on my knees, I receive you from
        from heaven.

In *Domani*, the two lovers surpass earthly limitations:

> *Non io tua, non tu mio: dello spazio: radendo*
> *   la terra con ali invisibili,*
> *sempre più lievi nell'aria, sempre più*
> *   immersi nel cielo,*
> *fino a quando la notte ci assuma ai suoi vasti*
> *   sepolcri di stelle.*

I not yours, you not mine: of space: grazing
    the earth with invisible wings,
ever lighter in air, ever more immersed
    in the sky,
till night shall assume us in its vast
    sepulchers of stars.

Il libro di Mara, along with *I canti dell'isola* (Songs of the Island, 1924) are considered the high point of Negri's poetic work. Through metrical and formal execution, they demonstrate the originality of her verse, which opens up to a more personal dimension almost prose-like and conversational, gains breath and becomes pliable. Her verse is impressionistic, spanned with bristling lyrics, with sudden igniting bursts and visionary flashes. Negri's poetry is made by going deep inside herself, in the travail of her childhood, in the solitude and the sleeplessness for an uncertain tomorrow, in the wounds of sorrow, in the misfortune that befalls each one of us. It expresses the hope and faith of an open heart in wait of a great love. In these rare moments of abandon and of happiness, the tone of her poetry lightens, and it is here that we glimpse the poet's solitary yearnings and intimate smiles, as in the late summer reveries of *Ode canicolare* (Summer Ode):

> *...trasfusa in gioia*
> *nel tuo biancore accecante,*
> *nelle tue nozze orgiastiche*
> *del calor con la luce,*
> *nelle tue notti stellate*
> *accese di rapidi lampi!*

> transfused in joy
> in your blinding whiteness,
> your lustful nuptials
> of heat with light,
> your star-filled nights
> lit with flashes of lightning!

The poem presents a series of sultry images, of "women lying half-naked in sweat on their beds," of a city "penetrated ailing with sun," of so much light dazzling the poet's eyes maybe forever, culminating in stanza five:

> *Ci amammo*
> *nella città felice,*
> *da lei posseduti*
> *e liberi in essa, padroni*
> *delle sue piazze uguali*
> *ad affocati deserti,*
> *de' tortuosi suoi vicoli*
> *pieni di baci e d'oblio,*

We loved one another
in the happy city,
by her possessed
and free in her, lords
of her squares that were
smoldering deserts,
of her winding alleys
filled with kisses and oblivion,

In a 1928 interview with Arturo Lanocita,[3] Negri recalls how she had always been fond of humble objects and of the weather: she loved the rain, the mist, the storms. She said that as a child she used to strain her ears to pick up the whistle of the wind or the rustling of the rain. She regarded her autobiographical novel, *Stella mattutina* (Morning Star, 1921) and *Il libro di Mara* as her least defective work. Talking about the very wide readership that her work enjoyed from the turn of the century, Negri mentioned the hundreds of letters she received from women who wrote to say, "...they feel, suffer and rejoice like me, and I have revealed them to themselves."

Negri was awarded the Mussolini Prize of 50,000 lire for artistic achievement, in 1931. In 1940, at age seventy, Negri was admitted into the Italian Academy of the Arts. She was the first woman to receive this distinction. Ironically, it solidified her ties with the Fascist State. She became the preeminent Italian poet, carrying out the role of an intellectual woman in a Fascist climate. Throughout the war years, she continued to write for the *Corriere della Sera*, and worked on two more collections, more spiritual and mystical than the others, *Fons amoris* (Fount of Love) and *Oltre* (Beyond), published posthumously. Ada Negri died in Milan on January 11th, 1945.

Interest in her work declined rapidly in the post-war period when her link with Mussolini and the Fascists

---

3.   *Scrittori del tempo nostro* (Milan: Ceschina).

was severely criticized. But, in recent articles the poet's association with Fascism is reconsidered: *Il Giornale.it*[4] states that the so called poetess of the Fourth State was actually a hostage of Fascism. The article goes on to describe how Negri was popular in her lifetime, one step away from the Nobel Prize in Literature, but fell into oblivion after her death. It asserts that perhaps her ideas were too close to the ideals of the traditional family and civic community of Fascism, nevertheless that she was actually a champion for women, and above all, for the poorest and most oppressed.

In another article, *Poesia di un atto di amore* (Poetry of an Act of Love),[5] Annamaria Gatti says that Ada Negri, at first exalted and then harshly cut off by the critics, neglected by anthologies, inconvenient and misunderstood, has been relegated to a "niche" in the literary world. Negri was a poet who lived intensely on her journey crossing two centuries, providing poetic moments that were solemn and precious.

> *Her heart opens to the world; it welcomes it and brings to it the cries and sighs of human frailty, of courage and spiritual yearning that she reads, interprets, and translates. In these times marked with superficiality, her poetry is still an instrument of redemption and progress, and it may benefit us to rediscover and love this woman and artist, so close and so human. Profound.*
>
> 🕊 Maria A. Costantini

Note: All citations of Italian origin are my own translation.

---

4. 03/08/2008.
5. *Città Nuova* 21 (2009)

Translator's Notes

I believe that to bring about effective literary translation one must have three loves: love for the creator of the original piece; love for language one, its primary language of expression; and love for language two, the language it was delivered into. The translator is not a conveyor of information; the translator is co-creator, since translation, like all creative writing, is an act of discovery. It necessitates in-depth reading and interpretation of the piece, and also willingness for painstaking revisions after the work has been put aside for a period of time, and then revisited with refreshed vision.

Choosing the best word requires awareness of its usage in the two target languages, set in different time periods. Garzanti Linguistica online is my invaluable resource for finding word connotations/denotations, etymologies, and archaic meanings. And, although my intention is to stay as loyal to the original as possible, in some cases, word-choice means compromise and a bit of betrayal.

Sound and movement in a poem also present a challenge. Italian is musical and offers ready rhymes. Trying to accomplish a similar pattern in English may result in drastic changes to syntax as well as manipulating vocabulary, running the risk of sounding contrived. Instead, I pay attention to tone, cadence, and rhythm and employ the use of slant rhyme and internal rhyme, alliteration and assonance.

The Italian use of inverted syntax, reflexive pronouns, passive voice, conditional past tenses, prepositions, gender pronouns, and strings of subordinate clauses, don't carry clearly into English without some alteration. Translating the conditional verb phrases, *Non sarebbe discesa la notte, non sarebbe venuto il domani* in *Il sole e l'ombra*, required deliberation: *There would have been no night, there would have been no tomorrow,* keeps the conditional but adds the English modifier "there." Another example is the appellation *in Ode canicolare, (Summer Ode): O mio geloso bene*, literally O my jealous love, is better interpreted as O my beloved season: the word *bene* here alludes to the season, not necessarily, yet, to a beloved man.

A sonnet I wrote when I began my work in translation sums it up:

Why Translate an Old Italian Poem?

Because when flavor and spice cross paths
with nuance from one tongue to another
you step outside yourself into the past

and taste the aphrodisiac of adventure.
You dash for Webster, Garzanti, Roget,
gaze at patterns of time-honored cultures,

retrace every footprint left on the page
and fit it to yours; do somersaults
and land in a new world. Stage by stage

a reflection of you will sneak through—caught
in the space between lines someone wrote
long ago—re-cast in the rhyme of their thoughts.

You steal the music from vowels that sing
to make an exiled poem a new-born thing.

Bibliography

This bibliography is indebted to Patrizia Zambon of the Dipartimento di Italianistica Università degli Studi di Padova and her website at http://www.maldura.unipd.it/italianistica/ALI/negri.html

Ada Negri's Works

Poetry
Fatalità. Milan: Treves, 1892.
Tempeste. Milan: Treves, 1896.
Maternità. Milan: Treves, 1904.
Dal profondo. Milan: Treves, 1910.
Esilio. Milan: Treves, 1914.
Il libro di Mara. Milan: Treves, 1919.
I canti dell'isola. Milan: Mondadori, 1925.
Vespertina. Milan: Mondadori, 1930.
Il dono. Milan: Mondadori, 1936.
Fons amoris. Milan: Mondadori, 1946.

Prose Stories
Le solitarie. Milan: Treves, 1917.
Orazioni. Milan: Treves, 1918.
Finestre alte. Milan: Mondadori, 1923.
Le strade. Milan: Mondadori, 1926.
Sorelle. Milan: Mondadori, 1929.
Di giorno in giorno. Milan: Mondadori, 1932.
Erba sul sagrato. Milan: Mondadori, 1939.
Oltre. Milan: Mondadori, 1947.

Novel
Stella mattutina. Milan: Mondadori, 1921.
—. Reprint ed. Milan: Mondadori, 1970.
—. Edited by Gianguido Scalfi e Anna Folli. Milan: La Vita Felice, 1995.
—. Edited by Maristella Lippolis e Maria Rosa Cutrufelli. Pescara: Tracce, 1995.

VARIOUS
Alessandrina Ravizza. Milan: Società Umanitaria Fondazione P. M. Loria,1915.

Traduzione di *Storia di Manon Lescaut e del Cavaliere di Grieux*, di Antoine François Prévost. Milan: Mondadori, 1931.

53 Art Poems of Ada Negri's were set to music by Ottorino Respighi and various other composers from 1911 through 1991. Catalogo del Polo BNCF. Biblioteca Centrale di Firenze.

LETTERS
"Nell'inverno del '42, tra i fuochi di guerra, una lettera a un'amica crocerossina." In *Avvenire* 11 January 1995.

Buzzi, Paolo. *Futurismo. Scritti, carteggi, testimonianze III*. Edited by Mario Morini and Giampaolo Pignatari. Milan: Biblioteca Comunale di Milano, 1983.

Comes, Salvatore. *Ada Negri. Da un tempo all'altro*. Milan: Mondadori, 1970.

Cremascoli, Luigi. *Lettere di Ada Negri nella Biblioteca Laudense*. In *Archivio storico lodigiano* 2.1 (1954).

—. *Lettere di Ada Negri in un carteggio privato*. In *Archivio storico lodigiano* 2.2 (1954).

Fraticelli, Vincenzo. *Incontri con Ada Negri*. Naples: Conti, 1954.

Gennaro, Salvatore. *Una piccola amicizia di Ada Negri*. Olgiate Olona (Varese): Grafica Olona, 1995.

Mondrone, Domenico. *Scrittori al traguardo*. Rome: La Civiltà cattolica, 1947.

Negri, Ada, and Paolo Buzzi. *Diorami lombardi. Carteggio (1896–1944)*. Edited by Barbara Stagnitti. Padova: Il Poligrafo, 2008.

Pea, Mauro. *Due anime. Testimonianze religiose e letterarie dal carteggio inedito Ada Negri — Federico Binaghi*. Lodi: Edizioni Besana Brianza, 1986.

Pignatari, Giampaolo. "*Carteggio Ada Negri — Paolo Buzzi.*" In *La Martinella di Milano* 34 (1980): 9–10.

Repossi, Cesare. *Cesare Angelini e Ada Negri. Incontri nella "rossa Pavia."* Pavia: Unitre, 1996.

BIBLIOGRAPHY OF CURATED WORKS SINCE 1970

L'appuntamento. In *Novelle d'autrice tra Otto e Novecento*. Edited by Patrizia Zambon. Rome: Bulzoni, 1998.

La Cacciatora e altri racconti. Edited by Antonia Arslan and Anna Folli. Milan: Scheiwiller, 1988.

La Cacciatora. In *Maestrine. Dieci racconti e un ritratto*. Edited by Vincenzo Campo. Palermo: Sellerio, 2000.

Le cartoline della nonna. Florence: Giunti e Nardini, 1973.

Clarissa. In *Novelle d'autrice tra Ottocento e Novecento*. Edited by Patrizia Zambon. Padova: Nuova Vita, 1987.

Mia giovinezza. Edited by Davide Rondoni. Milan: Rizzoli 1995.

Opere scelte. Edited by Elena Cazzulani and Gilberto Coletto. Lodi: Edizioni del Campus, 1984; Lodi: Lodigraf, 1988.

Opere scelte. Edited by Elena Cazzulani and Angela Gorini Santoli. Lodi: Il Pomerio, 1995.

Poesie. Edited by Silvio Raffo. Milan: Mondadori, 2002.

Translation of Antoine François Prévost. *Manon Lescaut*. Milan: ES, 1992.

ANTHOLOGIZED WORKS

Scrittrici d'Italia. Edited by Alma Forlani e Marta Savini. Rome: Newton Compton, 1991.

L'altro sguardo. Antologia delle poetesse del '900. Edited by Guido Davico Bonino and Paola Mastrocola. Milan: Mondadori, 1996.

Capriccio e coscienza. Scrittrici fra due secoli. Edited by Marino Biondi and Simona Moretti. Cesena: Società Editrice "Il Ponte Vecchio," 1997.

Miserabili in poesia. Criminali, marginali e vittime in versi contemporanei. Edited by Giovanni Greco and Davide Monda. Rome: Carocci, 2002.

SECONDARY WORKS SINCE 1970

Aa. Vv. *Incontri con Ada Negri*. Lodi: Associazione "Poesia, la Vita," 1995.

Aa. Vv. *Ada Negri: "Parole e ritmo sgorgan per incanto."* Pisa-Rome: Giardini Editori e Stampatori in Pisa, 2007.

Abbrugiati, Perle. "Les visages de la solitude dans les nouvelles d'Ada Negri." In *Les femmes écrivains en Italie aux XIXe et XXe siècles*. Centre Aixois de Recherches Italiennes. Aix-en-Provence: Publications de l'Université de Provence, 1993.

Angelini, Cesare. *Cronachette di letteratura contemporanea. 1919–1971*. Bologna: Boni, 1971.

—. *Trenta lettere*. Edited by Angelo Stella and Angelo Comini. Pavia: Almo Collegio Borromeo, 1981.

—. *I doni della vita. Lettere 1913–1976*. Edited by Angelo Stella and Anna Modena. Milan: Rusconi, 1985.

Arslan, Antonia. *Dame, galline e regine. La scrittura femminile italiana fra '800 e '900*. Milan: Guerini e Associati, 1998.

Baggio, Cristina. "Il mondo interiore di Ada visto attraverso i suoi epistolari." In *Sulle orme*.

Bellio, Anna. "Ada Negri e 'Poesia'." *Rivista di Letteratura italiana* 24.2 (2006).

Comes, Salvatore. *Ada Negri. Da un tempo all'altro*. Milan: Mondadori, 1970.

Cossu Maria Grazia. *Lo specchio di Venere. La scrittura autobiografica di Neera, Ada Negri, Marina Jarre e Lalla Romano*. Sassari: Editrice Democratica Sarda, 2009.

De Troja, Elisabetta. "Le lettere di Ada ad Ettore Patrizi." In *Sulle orme*.

—. "Solitudine e solitudini in Ada Negri." In *Le forme del narrare*. Florence: Polistampa, 2004.

Dolfi, Anna *et al. Memorie, autobiografie e diari nella letteratura italiana dell'Ottocento e del Novecento*. Pisa: Edizioni ETS, 2008.

Farina, Domenico. "L'ultima Ada Negri." In *L'Osservatore politico letterario* 16.11 (1970).

Farnetti, Monica. *Il giuoco del maligno. Il racconto fantastico nella letteratura italiana tra Otto e Novecento*. Florence: Vallecchi, 1988.

Folli, Anna. "Lettura di Ada Negri." In *Svelamento. Sibilla Aleramo: Una biografia intellettuale*. Edited by Annarita Buttafuoco. Milan: Feltrinelli, 1988.

—. "Sono ammalata d'anima. Ada Negri tra 'Fatalità' e 'Tempeste'." In *Les femmes — écrivains en Italie (1870–1920): Ordres et libertés*. Edited by Emmanuelle Genevois. Paris: Chroniques Italiennes — Université de la Sorbonne Nouvelle, 1994.

—. *Penne leggère. Neera, Ada Negri, Sibilla Aleramo. Scritture femminili italiane fra Otto e Novecento*. Milan: Guerini e Associati, 2000.

Gambaro, Elisa. "*Stella mattutina*. L'autobiografia regressiva di Ada Negri." In Dolfi, *Memorie*.

Giardini, Laura. "Le lettere di Ada Negri conservate nei Fondi del Gabinetto G.P. Vieusseux di Firenze. Il rapporto con 'Il Marzocco' e gli Orvieto." In *Sulle orme*.

Gorini Santoli, Angela. *Invito alla lettura di Ada Negri*. Milan: Mursia, 1995.

Mattalia, Daniele. *Ada Negri. Dal dilettantismo sociale all'estetismo piccolo borghese*. In *Novecento*. Milan: Marzorati, 1979.

Mazzoni, Cristina. "Difference, Repetition, and the Mother–Daughter Bond in Ada Negri." *Rivista di Studi italiani* 15.1 (1997).

—. "Impressive Cravings, Impressionable Bodies: Pregnancy and Desire from Cesare Lombroso to Ada Negri." *Annali d'Italianistica* 15.15 (1997).

Merry, Bruce. "Ada Negri: Social Injustice and an Early Italian Feminist." *Forum for Modern Language Studies*, 26.3 (1988).

Palombi Cataldi, Anna Maria. *Solaria. La Capri magica di Ada Negri*. Naples: Grimaldi & Cicerano, 1984.

Paris, Renzo. *Il mito del proletariato nel romanzo italiano*. Milan: Garzanti, 1977.

Pastorino, Nadia. "Il carteggio Ada Negri — Umberto Fracchia." In *Sulle orme*.
Pea, Mauro. *Ada Negri*. Milan: Mondadori, 1970.
Petrocchi, Giorgio. "Per il centenario di Ada Negri." In *Nuova Antologia* 105.2037 (1970).
Pickering-Iazzi, Robin. "The Politics of Gender and Genre in Italian Women's Autobiography of the Interwar Years." *Italica* 71.2 (1994).
Rasy, Elisabetta. *Ritratti di signora*. Milan: Rizzoli, 1995.
Ruschioni, Ada. *Dalla Deledda a Pavese*. Milan: Vita e Pensiero, 1977.
—. *Poesia e metafisica della luce*. Milan: Vita e Pensiero, 1987.
Sebastiani, Roberta. "La fortuna di Ada Negri nella letteratura russa." *Archivio storico lodigiano* 31.12 (1993).
Spaziani, Maria Luisa. *Donne in poesia*. Venezia: Marsilio, 1992.
Sulle orme di Ada Negri. Lodi: Associazione "Poesia, la Vita," 2003.
Tortora, Matilde. "Un'autobiografia trasposta. Le lettere inedite di Ada Negri a Eleonora Duse." In Dolfi, *Memorie*.
Ulivi, Ferruccio. "Il centenario di Ada Negri." *Galleria* 21.6 (1971).
Vené, Gian Franco. *Gli operai superuomini di Ada Negri*. In *Novecento*. Milan: Marzorati, 1979.
Wood, Sharon. *Italian Women's Writing 1860–1994*. London: Athlone, 1995.
Zaccaro, Vanna. *Shaharazàd si racconta: Temi e figure nella letteratura femminile del Novecento*. Bari: Palomar, 2005.
Zambon, Patrizia. "Ada Negri, 'La Cacciatora e altri racconti'." *Studi novecenteschi* 17.39 (1990).
—. *Letteratura e stampa nel secondo Ottocento*. Alessandria: Edizioni dell'Orso, 1993.
—. "Ada Negri scrittrice." In *Sulle orme*.
Zimbone, Croce. *Luigi Capuana, Salvatore Farina, Arturo Graf, Ada Negri: Segnalazioni critiche*. Catania: Greco, 1981.

The Book of Mara

Il sole e l'ombra

Sole di mezzogiorno, nel luglio felice,
sulla piazza deserta:

piazza lontana di città lontana, tu ed il tuo
uomo, e quello era il mondo.

Bianca nelle tua veste, bianca vibratile fiamma tu pure,
nell'abbaglio d'incendio dell'aria.

Bianco il tuo riso perduto nel riso di lui, fresco
di polla il tuo riso d'amore tra il vasto
fulgere ed ardere.

Non sarebbe discesa la notte, non sarebbe
venuto il domani, tua la luce, tuo l'uomo,
tuo il tempo.

Fermasti il tempo in pieno sull'ora solare
per cui in terra tu fosti divina:

il resto è ombra e polvere d'ombra.

The Sun and the Shadow

Noonday sun, that happy July,
  upon the empty square:

a distant square in a distant city, you and your
  man, and that was your world.

White in your dress, you too a pulsing white flame,
  in the blinding blaze of air.

White your laughter lost in his laughter,
  your laughter of love a fresh pool in the vast
  gleaming and burning.

There would have been no night, there would have been
  no tomorrow; yours the light, yours the man,
  yours the time.

You stopped all time that noon hour
  when on earth you were divine:

the rest is shadow and shadow dust.

Il ricordo

*Egli ti amò. Non avesti altro bene. Umìliati
e rendine grazie.*

*Nel silenzio dei giorni a venire, soli e gelidi
con te sola,*

*nelle strade piene di folla ove tu camminerai
come in mezzo ai deserti,*

*nella casa senza lampada, nel letto senza
riposo, nell'albe senza speranza,*

*non scordare il tuo amore, umìliati e rendine
grazie.*

*Ti sia presente in ogni minuto della vita che
ti rimane,*

*donna che non vedesti il cielo se non per lo
spiraglio di quell'amore.*

*Aggràppati alle sbarre, tendi il viso fra spranga
e spranga,*

*sàziati gli occhi di quel lembo d'azzurro, o
prigioniera dell'ombra.*

*Rammenta il corpo del tuo amante diritto
come un cipresso,*

*e la sua testa d'imperio che sopravanzava le
folle,*

*e il sùbito addolcirsi de' suoi occhi quand'egli
ti guardava,*

e la sua ferrea stretta che ti spezzava in due.

*Rammenta come egli seppe da te crearti più
bella e più giovine,*

*e dal cuore profondo strapparti il sol grido
di donna sincero in tua vita,*

Remembrance

He loved you. You had no other love. Be humble
 and give thanks.

In the silence of the coming days, lonely and cold
 with you alone,

in the crowded streets where you will walk
 as if amid deserts,

in the house without a lamp, in the bed without
 rest, in the dawns without hope,

do not forget your love, be humble and give
 thanks.

Keep it present every minute that remains
 of your life,

woman who saw not heaven if not for
 the glimpse of that love.

Cling to the bars; extend your face
 between them,

fill your eyes with that strip of sky,
 o prisoner of shadows.

Remember your lover's body straight
 as a cypress,

and his imperious head that stood above
 the crowd,

and the sudden sweetness in his eyes when he
 looked at you,

and his tight embrace that broke you in two.

Remember how he learned, from you, to make you
 younger and more beautiful,

and to tear from deep in your heart the only real
 woman's scream of your life,

*e vestirti e nutrirti d'amore e toglierti a tutto
che non fosse amore.*

*E come egli seppe anche farti soffrire nel
corpo e nell'anima,*

*e come tu amasti e godesti il dolore che ti
venne da lui:*

*e che una volta un suo morso t'aperse nel
labbro una piccola piaga,*

*e tu guarir non volevi di quella dolcissima
stimmate*

*per cui tutto serbavi in tua bocca il sapor del
tuo amore.*

*Sapore di sangue; e il tuo amore spirava in
un fiotto di sangue*

*che ti sprizzò sino agli occhi; e tu, tu sei
ancor viva.*

*Quanto sangue in quel grande corpo! Ora
è tuo, passò tutto in te.*

*Ne hai turgide e inferme le vene, ne hai
rombo perenne alle tempie.*

*Bolle ed urge per forza compressa, ti riempie
il cuore di clamanti voci.*

*Che farai tu di quel sangue?... Pianto per
piangere il tuo morto, parola per celebrarlo.*

*Viatico per il cammino, ché ancor camminare
tu devi; e nutrimento per la memoria.*

*Sangue ardente, sangue d'amore, non ne andrà
spersa neppure una stilla:*

*fino a quando il suo peso ti abbatta con la
faccia contro la terra,*

*e dire tu possa con l'ultimo soffio: "Signore,
la tua serva è qui."*

and to clothe and nourish you with love and take
  you away from all that was not love.

And how he also knew the way to make you suffer
  in body and soul,

and how you loved and took joy in the suffering
  that came from him:

like the time his bite cut
  a small wound in your lip,

and you didn't want to heal from that sweetest
  stigmata

by which you held in your mouth the full taste
  of your love.

Taste of blood; and your love was dying
  in a spurt of blood

that shot up to your eyes; and you, you are
  still alive.

So much blood in that great body! Now it is yours;
  all of it flowed into you.

From it your veins are swollen and sick; from it
  the constant rumble at your temples.

Boiling and urging from a force compressed, it fills
  your heart with clamoring voices.

What will you make of that blood? Tears
  to weep for your dead man, words to praise him.

Provisions for your journey, for you have more
  traveling to do; and food for your memory.

Ardent blood, blood of love, not even a drop
  will be wasted:

until the day its weight will pull you down,
  face to the ground,

and you'll be able say with your final breath: "Lord,
  your maidservant is here."

La Crocifissa

Confitta è alla croce e non la darebbe per
un letto di bianchi giacinti:

un chiodo nel palmo destro, uno nel palmo
sinistro, uno nei piedi avvinti.

Il primo è l'amore che a te la condusse
senz'altra forza che per amarti,

l'altro è il dolore che in vita la serba
senz'altra voce che per chiamarti,

il terzo è il ricordo di tutti gl'istanti sbocciati
per voi nei giardini del sole:

or che sei morto nessun la compianga: sol
la sua croce ella ama, sol la sua croce vuole.

Quando la sete le spacca le labbra, beve alle
tue labbra il gran sorso che sazia:

quando la morte le diaccerà il cuore, morrà
in te, nel segno della tua grazia.

Crucified

She is nailed to the cross and would not trade it
   for a bed of white hyacinths:

a nail in the right palm, one in the left palm,
   one in the feet bound together.

The first is the love that led her to you
   by no force other than to love you,

the second is the sorrow that keeps her alive
   with no voice other than to call you,

the third is the memory of all the moments blossomed
   for you in the gardens of the sun:

now that you are dead may no one pity her: she loves
   only her cross, she wants only her cross.

When thirst splits her lips, she drinks
   from your lips the long sip that satisfies:

when death freezes her heart, she will perish
   in you, in the sign of your grace.

Ada Negri

Apparizione

Entrasti improvviso, lasciando spalancata la porta sui campi.

Gran vampa di sole a meriggio con soffio di spazio entrò nella stanza con te.

Volle la donna moverti incontro; ma abbaglio, timore, tremore la vinsero.

Mai fino allora ella aveva veduto l'uomo ed il sole risplendere a paro.

Così alto eri, che ti curvasti per toccarle una spalla con la mano.

Così compatto il silenzio, che le parole non dette si scolpiron solenni nell'aria.

Fin che la donna vivrà, quelle parole dentro il suo cuore, e la tua mano sulla sua spalla.

Fin che la donna vivrà, tu a paro col sole, nel suo ricordo.

Apparition

You came in suddenly, leaving
  the door to the fields wide open.

A blaze of midday sun with a breath of open air
  entered the room with you.

The woman wanted to move toward you; but dazzle,
  fear, tremor overcame her.

Not until then had she seen a man and the sun
  shine as equals.

So tall were you, you bent down to touch
  her shoulder with your hand.

So dense the silence, the words not spoken
  solemnly carved the air.

As long as the woman shall live, so will those words
  in her heart, and your hand on her shoulder.

As long as the woman shall live, you will equal the sun
  in her memory.

Ada Negri

Sinfonia azzurra

Venne in cerca di te
nella calda notte, lungo le strade dai fanali azzurri.
Tutte le strade, allora, la notte erano azzurre
come le vie dei cieli,
e il volto amato
non si vedeva: si sentiva in cuore.
E ti trovò, o dolcezza, nell'ombra
casta, velata d'un vapor di stelle.
Fra quel tremolio d'astri
discesi in terra,
in quell'azzurro di due firmamenti
l'uno a specchio dell'altro, ella ella pure
rispecchiò in te l'anima sua notturna.
E ti seguì con passo di bambina
senza sapere, senza vedere, tacita e fluida.
E allor che il giorno apparve
con fresco riso roseo su l'immenso turchino,
non trovò più se stessa
per ritornare.

Blue Symphony

She came looking for you,
in the hot night, along the streets with blue lamplights.
All the streets were blue at night, then,
like the roads of the heavens,
and your beloved face
was not visible: she felt it in her heart.
And she found you, o sweetness, cast
in darkness, veiled in a mist of stars.
In that glimmer of stars
descended on earth,
in the azure of two firmaments
mirroring each other, she, she too
saw her nocturnal soul reflected in you.
And she followed you with the step of a young girl
without knowing, without seeing, tacit and fluid.
And when daylight appeared
with roseate laughter on the deep immense blue,
she never found herself again
to return.

Quel giorno

Quando tu le camminasti accanto con
elastico passo d'amore

sulle rive del rapido fiume verdeargento fra
le praterie.

Tutto in quel giorno era verdeargento, tutto
era infanzia, speranza e bontà,

perché tu le camminavi accanto, limpido
come un fanciullo nel balenante riso.

Ed ella al tuo braccio piegava al tuo ritmo
quale barca leggera sull'onda:

ella, femmina piccola e profonda, nata
a seguire, nata a blandire, nata a risplendere
della tua luce.

E quello fu il vostro giorno, il giorno di festa
della santa vita,

riflesso in serenità verdeargentea nei giorni
trascorsi e nei giorni a venire.

E non vale che tu ora sia morto ed ella
distrutta nel solo perché d'esser viva,

se la gioia d'un giorno fu in te, uomo della
tua donna: in lei, donna del suo uomo.

That Day

You walked beside her with the pliant
  step of love

along the banks of the fast-flowing river, silver-green
  among meadows.

Everything that day was silver-green, everything
  was childhood, hope and goodness,

because you walked beside her, limpid
  like a child in your dazzling smile.

And she on your arm folded to your rhythm
  as a light boat on a wave:

she, a woman small and profound, born to follow,
  born to cajole, born to shine
  of your light.

And that was your day, the feast-day
  of blessed life,

reflected in the silver-green serenity of days
  past and of days to come.

And it doesn't matter that now you are dead and she
  destroyed only because she's alive,

if one day's joy was in you, man of your
  woman: in her, woman of her man.

Ada Negri

Notturno nuziale

Quando tu venisti, una notte, verso il suo
letto, al buio,

e le dicesti, piano, già sopra di lei: "Non ti
vedo, ti sento."

E la ghermisti con artiglio d'aquila, e tutta
la costringesti nella tua forza,

riplasmandola in te con tal furore ch'ella
perdette il senso di esistere.

E uno solo in due bocche fu il rantolo e misto
fu il sangue e fu il ritmo perfetto,

e dal balcone aperto la notte guardava con
l'occhio d'una sola stella rossastra,

e il sonno che seguì parve la morte, e immoti
come cadaveri la tristezza dell'ombra vi
vegliò sino all'alba.

Wedding Nocturne

When you came, one night, to her bed,
  in the dark,

and told her, softly, already upon her: "I don't
  see you, I feel you."

And you gripped her with the claw of an eagle,
  and compelled all of her with your strength,

re-molding her to you with such fury that she lost
  her sense of existence.

And from two mouths came one gasp, and fused
  was their blood, perfect their rhythm,

and from the open balcony night looked on
  with the eye of a single red star,

and the sleep that followed resembled death and over you,
  immobile as cadavers, the sadness of shadows
  kept watch until dawn.

IL RISVEGLIO

Quando il canto del gallo segò il cielo, ed
ella ancor nel sonno a te sorrise, o amato.

L'uno dall'altro nasceste allora, in purità di
corpo, in purità di spirito.

O voi beati, non espressi da grembo di madre,
ma dalla meraviglia del vostro amore!

E vi levaste con atti limpidi, ed il primo
mattino del mondo con voi si levò.

E nuovi furono agli occhi vostri i rosei cirri
del cielo specchiati nei fiori dei peschi,

nuova l'erba intrisa di guazza, fresca alle mani
come un lavacro,

divina in voi la dolcezza di scoprirvi un nell'altro presenti e viventi,

con anima per amare,

labbra per baciare,

voce per benedire.

The Awakening

When the crow of the rooster sawed the sky
  and she still asleep smiled at you, o beloved.

You were born from each other then, in purity
  of body, in purity of spirit.

O blessed ones, not delivered from a mother's
  womb, but from the wonder of your love!

And you arose with clarity, and the first
  morning of the world rose with you.

And new to your eyes were the pink cirrus clouds
  of the sky reflected in peach blossoms,

new the grass drenched with dew, fresh to the hands
  like a cleansing,

divine in you the sweetness of discovering one
  in the other, present and alive,

with a soul to love,

lips to kiss,

voice to bless.

Ada Negri

Trasumanazione

Quando il tuo corpo immoto fu tolto ai suoi
  occhi bruciati dal pianto,

e solo aria per essa tu fosti, e il tuo amore
  con te si diffuse nel mistero degli elementi.

In ogni atomo ella ti respira, dio de' suoi
  cinque sensi;

e tu penetri il corpo mortale e tu penetri
  l'anima eterna

come una freccia di sole fra nube e nube
  discende a ferire la terra.

Di quel che offende la carne caduca nulla,
  più nulla può colpirla,

tua com'ella è nella luce e nello spazio,
  nell'altezza e nella profondità.

Di giorno, di notte, presente, assoluto,
  o amore invisibile, o amore universo,

tu l'assorbi come allora che il tuo amplesso
  rapinava tutto di lei,

dal pollice del piede contratto alla radice
  delle schiumanti chiome.

Ascesa anch'ella al tuo rogo di morte,
  per essere assolta e purificata,

per riaverti dal fuoco, dall'aria, dagli astri,
  da ogni bellezza creata.

Transhumanation

When your motionless body was removed from her
  tear-burnt eyes,

for her you became only air, and your love
  was diffused with you in the mystery of the elements.

In every atom she breathes you in, god of her five
  senses;

and you penetrate her mortal body and you penetrate
  her eternal soul

the way an arrow of sun shoots down between cloud
  and cloud to wound the earth.

Of what there is to harm the fragile flesh nothing,
  nothing more can strike it,

for it is yours as she is in light and space, altitude
  and depth.

By day, by night, present, absolute, o invisible
  love, o universal love,

you absorb her like the times when your embrace
  ravaged all of her,

from the toes of her contracted feet to the roots
  of her flowing hair.

She too ascended to your funeral pyre,
  to be forgiven and purified,

to reclaim you from the fire, from the air,
  from the stars, from every beauty created.

ADA NEGRI

LETTERE

*Brevi erano le tue lettere, precise, tutte muscolo
   e nervo,
di mano più usa al compasso, alla squadra,
   al gesto del duro comando.
Dicevan le semplici cose con semplici nude
   parole;
ma due ne portavano in fine, due, sempre le
   stesse: "Sei mia."
E quando ella giungeva, leggendo, al termine
   noto,
s'abbandonava all'indietro, vuotata del sangue,
   morente d'amore.
Ombre violacee intorno alla socchiusa bocca,
   all'affilato naso —
precipitoso palpito delle vene gonfiate alle
   tempie alla gola —
cecità delle palpebre, tensione delle mascelle
   nel desiderio —
faccia di donna agonizzante in estasi, tu non
   la vedesti, nessuno la vide. Era sola.*

*Ora, ogni notte, la donna che più non vorrebbe
   esser viva
nel vuoto della sua casa che ha odore di
   cenere spenta
scioglie un pacco di lettere legato con un
   nastro nero.
E legge; e, giunta al termine ben noto che a
   ognuna è sigillo,
ancor s'abbandona all'indietro, vuotata del
   sangue, morente d'amore.
Così, dalla tomba, con dura predace potenza
   di sillabe scritte
tu l'imprigioni, o scomparso, tu la possiedi
   così.*

Letters

Your letters were brief, precise, all muscle
    and nerve,
in a hand more apt for the compass, the square,
    the tough wave of command.
They said simple things with bare simple
    words;
but for two closing words, two, always
    the same: "You're mine."
And reading them, when she came to the familiar
    end,
she leaned back in abandon, drained of blood,
    dying of love.
Violet shadows around her half-open mouth,
    her thin nose —
a furious throb in her veins swelling
    at the temples, at the throat —
eyelids shut tight, jaws tense
    with desire —
the face of an agonizing woman in rapture; you
    didn't see her, no one saw her. She was alone.

Now, every night, the woman who no longer wants
    to live
in the emptiness of her home that smells
    of dead ashes,
unties a parcel of letters bound
    in black ribbon.
She reads; and, when she comes to the familiar
    ending that seals each one,
she still leans back in abandon, drained
    of blood, dying of love.
So, from the tomb, with the predacious power
    of written words,
you imprison her, o vanished one, you possess her
    thus.

Il silenzio

Ella anche ti amava nelle tue collere taciturne

*quando tu ti chiudevi in te stesso come in
   un'armatura irta di punte,*

*come dietro una porta di bronzo serrata con
   sette chiavi.*

*Senza protesta subiva, tremando nel cuore,
   i tuoi duri silenzi,*

*solo seguendo il tuo passo con passo
   vellutato d'ombra,*

*solo osando furtive carezze con piccole mani
   leggere*

*più soave quanto più grave il giogo d'amore
   calcato da te.*

Ma adesso la tua collera da troppo tempo dura,

ma perdute sono le chiavi che serran la porta di bronzo,

*ma invano la piccola mano va scuotendo dì
   e notte il battente,*

*ma senza pietà, senza fine è il silenzio del tuo
   sepolcro.*

The Silence

She loved you also in your quiet rages

when you shut yourself inside yourself as if
   in an armor bristling with spikes,

as if behind a bronze door locked with
   seven keys.

Without protest she endured with trembling heart
   your long harsh silences,

only trailing your steps with the velvet step
   of a shadow,

only daring furtive caresses with her small light
   hands,

the more tender the more heavily you trampled on
   your yoke of love.

But now your rage has lasted too long,

but lost are the keys that lock the bronze door,

but in vain the small hand goes to knock on the door
   day and night,

but without pity, without end is the silence
   of your sepulcher.

O TARDI VENUTO

O tardi venuto, nel tempo in cui la porta si chiude

*sulla speranza, e l'ombra discende dagli alti
cipressi:*

*o in così rapido modo scomparso, che parve
il tuo avvento*

*un sogno, e ancor mi domando nel cuore s'io
vaneggiai:*

*come or vuoi tu ch'io sappia condurre i miei
passi nel mondo*

*senz'acqua per la mia sete, senz'aria pel mio
respiro?*

*Taccio; ma ti risuscito nella tua carne
mortale*

con la bellezza rude che folle mi rese di te.

*Ed io cammino appesa al tuo braccio, e mi
stringo al tuo cuore;*

*e se dir t'odo il mio nome, impallidisco come
chi muore.*

O Latecomer

You came at the time the door closes

on hope, and darkness descends from tall
  cypresses:

o so swiftly you vanished, that it seemed
  your arrival

was a dream, and I still ask my heart if I was
  delirious:

how do you expect me to make
  my way in the world now

without water for my thirst, without air for
  my breath?

I am silent; but I revive you to your mortal
  flesh

with its rugged beauty that once made me mad about you.

And I walk draped on your arm, pressing myself
  to your heart;

and if I hear you calling my name, I turn pale like
  someone dying.

Il figlio

La donna che or vive nascosta come una
bestia ferita nel covo

e più non osa guardare il sole perché i tuoi
occhi son chiusi per sempre,

mai consolarsi potrà che da te non sia nato
al suo grembo un bambino,

un bambino che t'assomigli, che sia tuo, che
sia te, carne e spirito, forza e bellezza.

Ti bacerebbe su quella bocca, ti respirerebbe
in quel fresco respiro,

creata e creatrice, amante e madre in ardore
inesausto di dono.

Se tu fecondato l'avessi, calmo sarebbe il suo
viscere sacro,

nel necessario riposo del compiuto travaglio
di vita.

Serva felice ti fu, serva ancor ti sarebbe
adorando il tuo figlio,

mangiando ella il pane raffermo perch'egli
gioisca di frutta succose,

pestando ella i sassi e gli spini perch'egli
scavalli in letizia su l'erbe fiorite.

La donna che or fissa con occhi sbarrati le
vuote sue mani nel grembo riverse

compose il bimbo che non le nacque sul tuo
cuore che non batte più.

The Son

The woman who now lives hidden like a wounded
 animal in its lair

and no longer dares look at the sun because your
 eyes are closed forever,

will never be consoled that her womb did not give birth
 to a son by you,

a child who would resemble you, who would be yours,
 who would be you, flesh and spirit, strength and beauty.

On that mouth she would be kissing you, in that fresh
 breath breathe you in,

she, created and creator, lover and mother, in the inexhaustible
 fervor of giving.

Had you fathered him, her sacred womb would be
 at peace

in the necessary rest when life's labor
 is done.

Happy to be your servant, she would still be
 your servant by worshipping your son,

by eating stale bread so he may enjoy
 succulent fruit,

by crushing rocks and thorns so he may leap
 in merriment across prairies in bloom.

The woman who now stares with eyes wide open
 at her empty hands reversed on her lap

laid the child she didn't bear upon your
 heart that beats no more.

ACCETTAZIONE

*Accetto la cosa tremenda, per seguire la tua
   volontà.*

*Quando mai, nel tempo felice, io ti disobbedii,
   signore?*

*Accetto, poiché l'hai voluto, d'essere cieca
   delle tue pupille,*

sorda della tua voce, mutilata nelle tue membra,

*e non bestemmio e non urlo e m'inginocchio
   con viso a terra.*

*Arerò il campo in tua vece, seminerò in tua
   vece il grano,*

*con le mani di carezza e d'ala che tu come
   reliquie adoravi;*

*e quando le spighe mature vampeggeranno
   nel solleone*

*le mieterò io stessa con la falce che t'ha
   mietuto.*

*Poi siederò su un mannello, rivolto il viso
   alla nascente luna,*

*calma attendendo il fiorire nell'aria del canto
   dell'Ave*

*per dirti: "Amico, finito è il giorno, compiuto
   il travaglio, l'ora di Dio suona:*

concedimi, concedimi

*riudir la voce, rivedere il volto, sorriderti
   accanto in eterno."*

Acceptance

I accept this dreadfulness, in order to follow
  your will.

When, in happy times, did I ever disobey you,
  lord?

I accept, since you have willed it, to be blind
  of your pupils,

deaf to your voice, crippled in your limbs,

and I don't curse and I don't scream and I kneel
  face to the ground.

I will plough the field in your place, I will sow
  the grain in your place,

with my caressing wing-like hands you
  adored like relics;

and when ripened wheat-stalks blaze
  in the noonday sun

I will reap them myself with the scythe
  that reaped you.

Then I will sit on a sheaf, my face turned
  to the crescent moon,

calmly waiting for the air to bloom with the song
  of the Ave

to tell you: "Friend, day is done, my work
  is accomplished, the hour of God strikes:

grant me, grant me

to hear your voice again, to see your face again, to smile
  beside you for eternity."

ASCENSIONE

*E tu che farai, anima, per renderti in vita
degna del tuo morto?*

*Saprai d'ogni colpa mondarti, d'ogni viltà
liberarti,*

*e vivere in ardente purezza e comporti in
ardente umiltà?*

*Saprai continuare il tuo morto nel cammino
del sogno e dell'opera,*

*testimoniarlo in fede con voce e con mano
santificata,*

*farne midollo per l'ossa tue e d'altri, sangue
vermiglio pel cuore d'altri e tuo?*

*Pòggiati alla sua ombra, poi ch'è più salda
delle colonne:*

*ricevi in te il suo spirito come la terra il seme
per ansia feconda di mèsse:*

*fino alle nozze supreme che vi attendon
nell'ora di Dio*

al tempio azzurro delle Sette Stelle.

Ascension

And what will you do, soul, to become worthy
  in life of your dead man?

Will you know how to cleanse yourself of sin,
  free yourself of evil,

live in fervent purity and act in fervent
  humility?

Will you know how to continue the dream and work
  of your dead man,

bear him witness in faith with sanctified voice
  and hand,

make of him marrow for your bones and others', vermillion
  blood for your heart and others'?

Lean upon his shadow, for it is more solid
  than a pillar:

receive his spirit as the ground the seed
  with the fertile eagerness of harvest:

until the supreme nuptials that await you
  in the hour of God

at the blue temple of the Seven Stars.

Il vuoto

*Oggi ti cerco e non ti trovo, non sei né in
me né presso di me.*

*Né so qual colpa io abbia commessa, perché
tu mi punisca nella luce della tua presenza.*

*O signore, se tu m'abbandoni, che vuoi che
avvenga della tua creatura?*

*La mendica che stende la mano trova pur
sempre la mano soave nel porgerle aiuto.*

*Di lei più nuda e più cieca, io che brancolo
al buio dopo averti perduto, signore.*

*Andrò sino al cancello dell'orto: forse ti sei
nascosto dietro al gruppo dei tre pinastri.*

*Andrò sino in fondo alla strada: forse mi
attendi al limite dei campi.*

*Andrò sino alla riva del mare: forse la tua
voce mi chiamerà dalle acque.*

*Andrò sino agli abissi dei cieli: forse dentro
una tomba stellare la tua stretta mi riavvinghierà.*

The Void

Today I search for you and do not find you; you're neither
   in me nor beside me.

Nor do I know what wrong I've done, that you
   would deprive me of the light of your presence.

O lord, if you abandon me, what do you think
   will become of your creature?

Even the beggar who holds out her hand always finds
   a gentle hand offering her help.

More naked, blinder than she, I grope
   in the dark after having lost you, lord.

I will go as far as the garden gate: maybe you
   are hiding behind the cluster of three pines.

I will go as far as the end of the road: maybe you
   are waiting for me at the edge of the fields.

I will go as far as the shore of the sea: maybe your
   voice will call me from the waters.

I will go as far as the abyss of the skies: maybe inside
   a tomb of stars your grip will clutch me again.

Ada Negri

LA FOLLIA

*Una foglia cadde dal platano, un fruscio
scosse il cuore del cipresso:*

sei tu che mi chiami.

*Occhi invisibili succhiellano l'ombra,
s'infiggono in me come chiodi in un muro:*

sei tu che mi guardi.

*Mani invisibili le spalle mi toccano, verso
l'acque dormenti del pozzo mi attirano:*

sei tu che mi vuoi.

*Su su dalle vertebre diacce con pallidi taciti
brividi la follia sale al cervello:*

sei tu che mi penetri.

*Più non sfiorano i piedi la terra, più non pesa
il corpo nell'aria, via lo porta l'oscura
vertigine:*

sei tu che mi travolgi, sei tu.

Folly

A leaf fell from the sycamore, a rustle
  shook the heart of the cypress:

it is you calling me.

Invisible eyes bore through the shadows,
  drive into me like nails in a wall:

it is you watching me.

Invisible hands touch my shoulders, pulling
  me toward the sleeping waters of the well:

it is you wanting me.

Up up my icy vertebrae in pale quiet shivers,
  folly climbs to my brain:

it is you going through me.

No longer do my feet touch the ground. No longer
  does my body weigh on the air, seized by
  this dark giddiness:

it is you sweeping me away, it is you.

Grido

Quando tu mi stringevi, divino carnefice,
  smorta e demente fra le tue tanaglie,

pregavo nel tremito: "Uccidimi."

Sarei morta di te, sarei morta di gioia,
  lampeggiando i miei denti nel supremo
  inestinguibile riso.

Tu invece sei morto. Tanaglie ti furon le
  braccia della terribile che non ha volto,

e che tu amasti più di me, più di me.

Come puoi ora uccidermi? Ché più a lungo
  io non posso curvarmi a questa condanna
  dei giorni.

Torna una volta, col grande tuo corpo in
  ansito in vampa sul mio prostrato pallore.

Afferrami come facevi quand'io non ero che
  amore tremante dinanzi al tuo amore.

Annientami dentro di te, che mi sien tolti
  i sensi, che mi si rompa il cuore.

Cry

Whenever you gripped me, wan and demented,
  tight in your pincers, divine executioner,

I prayed in tremor: "Kill me."

I would have died of you; I would have died of joy,
  flashing my teeth in the supreme inextinguishable
  smile.

Instead, you died. For you the arms of the
  terrible one who has no face were pincers,

and it was she you loved more than me, more than me.

How can you kill me now? That I can no longer
  bow to this condemnation
  of days.

Come back just one time, with your great body
  panting on fire over mine, prostrate and pale.

Grab me as you did when I was but
  a trembling love before your love.

Annihilate me inside you, that my senses
  may steal away, that my heart may break.

Il muro

Alto è il muro che fiancheggia la mia strada,
e la sua nudità rettilinea si prolunga
nell'infinito.

Lo accende il sole come un rogo enorme, lo
imbianca la luna come un sepolcro.

Di giorno, di notte, pesante, inflessibile, sento
il tuo passo di là dal muro.

So che sei lì, e mi cerchi e mi vuoi, pallido
nel pallore marmoreo che avevi l'ultima
volta ch'io ti vidi.

So che sei lì, ma porta non trovo da schiudere,
breccia non posso scavare.

Parallela al tuo passo io cammino, senz'altro
udire, senz'altro seguire che questo solo
richiamo,

sperando incontrarti alla fine, guardarti beata
nel viso, svenirti beata sul cuore.

Ma il termine sempre è più lungi, e in me non
v'è fibra che non sia stanca;

ed il tuo passo di là dal muro si scande a
martello sul battito delle mie arterie.

The Wall

High is the wall that flanks my road,
  and its rectilinear bareness extends
  into infinity.

The sun lights it like an enormous pyre, the moon
  whitens it like a sepulcher.

By day, by night, I hear your heavy, inflexible step
  on the other side of the wall.

I know you're there, pale with the marble
  pallor you had the last time I saw you,
  looking for me and wanting me.

I know you're there; but I can't find a door
  to open, no breach I can dig through.

I walk parallel to your step, if only to hear,
  if only to follow its call,

hoping to meet you at the end, to look at you
  with bliss, with bliss to faint upon your heart.

But the end grows ever more distant, and there's
  no fiber in me that's not weary;

and your step on the other side of the wall pounds
  like a hammer on the pulse of my arteries.

Incantesimo

*Vanno per vie deserte tagliate a metà dalla
   luna*

*i due amanti felici d'amarsi, certi d'essere
   uniti in eterno:*

*fianco contro fianco, spalla contro spalla, e
   pur li separa l'aria impalpabile:*

*cuore contro cuore, amore contro amore,
   e pur li separa la Vitamorte:*

vicinissimi,

lontanissimi.

*Seguono il nastro d'ombra, perchè troppo
   chiara e curiosa è la luna*

*che sparge diamanti sui tetti, che rende i
   muri intenti come volti,*

*trae brividi bianchi dall'acque del canale
   sorpreso nel sonno,*

*pone sulle cimase e sulle porte misteriose
   parole di splendore.*

*Così limpida e casta la luna, così nera e
   vellutata l'ombra:*

*fascia di lente carezze intrisa di un denso
   sentore di tigli.*

*Ed egli bisbiglia: "Domani!" Ed ella
   risponde: "Sempre!"*

*E vanno, e non sanno che un d'essi, il più
   forte, preso è già nella tela di ragno tessuta
   per lui dalla morte:*

*spalla contro spalla, amore contro amore,
   effimeri nell'attimo, illusi d'eternità,*

vicinissimi,

lontanissimi.

Enchantment

They go down deserted roads cut in half
  by the moon

the two lovers happy to love, certain they'll be
  together for all time:

side by side, shoulder to shoulder, and yet
  the impalpable air divides them:

heart to heart, love to love,
  and yet Life-Death divides them:

so very near,

so very far.

They follow the ribbon of darkness, because
  of the too clear and curious moon

that spreads diamonds on rooftops,
  turns walls into watchful faces,

draws white shivers from the waters
  of the canal surprised in its sleep,

places mysterious words of splendor
  on moldings and doors.

So clear and pure is the moon, so black
  and velvet the darkness:

a sash of slow caresses infused with a dense
  fragrance of lime-trees.

And he whispers: "Tomorrow!" And she
  answers: "Always!"

And they go, unknowing that one of them,
  the stronger one, is already caught
  in a web spun for him by death:

shoulder to shoulder, love to love,
  ephemeral in the moment, illusive of eternity,

so very near,

so very far.

Il costruttore

*Gioia del giorno in cui egli t'addusse fra
gli uomini rudi alzanti a' suoi cenni le case
degli uomini,*

*e dinanzi agli artieri obbedienti e dinanzi alla
vinta materia tu lo vedesti imperatore e re.*

*Bolliva la liquida calce a specchio del solleone,
salivano i massi granitici entro i carrelli delle
alate gru,*

*stridevan catene, lucevano sbarre, con riso
squillante cantava il lavoro all'azzurro*

*nella rete d'acciaio e cemento, dall'alto delle
impalcature vertiginose.*

*Fibra per fibra, membro per membro, la casa
degli uomini andava radicandosi nella terra,
inquadrandosi nell'aria;*

*e tutto intorno, scheletri di muraglie,
spranghe e carrucole, muscoli e tendini, peso
volume sforzo di materia in travaglio,*

*tutto obbediva a un sol gesto, tutto era
vivente e movente, perché il Capo, là in
mezzo, viveva.*

*E tu, femmina piccola e profonda, perduta-
mente amasti il tuo padrone in lui:*

*e pur di appartenergli nel ritmo dell'opera,
invocasti la sorte del più misero e lacero
portatore di ghiaia.*

*Ma tu eri bella e tenevi sul petto una rosa,
una rosetta dal cuore giallo*

come una fiamma raccolta, come una gemma di sole,

*e gliela offristi: in quel gesto, presso a lui re,
sovrana.*

The Builder

Joyful the day he brought you among
  the rugged men erecting men's houses
  to his commands,

and before the obedient sappers and before
  the conquered matter you saw him as emperor and king.

Liquid lime boiled, mirroring the dog-day sun,

granite boulders rose inside the carts of
  winged cranes,

chains creaked, crossbars gleamed, with shrill laughter
  labor sang to the sky

in the network of steel and cement, from high up
  the dizzying scaffolds.

Fiber by fiber, limb by limb, the men's house
  was taking root in the earth,
  framing itself in the air;

and all around, skeletons of walls, rods
  and pulleys, muscles and tendons, weight
  volume exertion of matter at work,

everything obeying a single nod, everything
  alive and in motion, because the Leader, there in
  the middle, was alive.

And you, female, small and intense, desperately
  loved the master in him:

and to be a part of him in the rhythm of work,
  you pleaded for the lot of the most destitute
  and wretched gravel-carrier.

But you were beautiful and wore a rose on your breast,
  a small rose with a yellow heart

folded in like a flame, like a bud of sun,

and you offered it to him: in that gesture, beside him,
  king, you were queen.

Anniversario

Non chiamarmi, non dirmi nulla,
non tentare di farmi sorridere.
Oggi io sono come la belva
che si rintana per morire.

Abbassa la lampada, copri il fuoco,
che la stanza sia come una tomba.
Lascia ch'io mi rannicchi nell'angolo
con la testa sulle ginocchia.

L'ore si spengano nel silenzio.
Salga in torbide onde l'angoscia
e m'affoghi: altro non chiedo
che di perdere la conoscenza.

Ma non m'è dato. Quel volto,
quel riso l'ho sempre davanti.
Giorno e notte il ricordo m'è uncíno
confitto nella carne viva.

Forse morire io non potrò
mai: condannata in eterno
a vegliare il mio strazio in me,
piangendo con occhi senza palpebre.

Anniversary

Don't call me, say nothing,
　don't try to make me smile.
　Today I'm like a wild beast
　back in its lair to die.

Dim the lamp, cover the fire,
　so the room is like a tomb.
　Let me huddle in the corner
　with my head upon my knees.

May the hours fade into silence.
　May anguish rise in turbid waves
　and drown me: I ask for nothing else
　than to lose my senses.

But to me it's not granted. That face,
　that laughter, always before me.
　Day and night their memory's a hook
　embedded in my flesh.

I may never be able
　to die: condemned for all time
　to wake over my torment
　weeping with lidless eyes.

Ada Negri

〰 *(I SOGNI)*

La mano

Ti svegliasti avanti l'alba, in affanno ed
in brivido, perché avevi sognato il tuo
morto.

Sognato l'avevi com'era in sua vita, e pur
chiuso in un manto inviolabile d'ombra.

Non lo vedevi, sì lo sentivi: sentivi la sua
grande mano sopra di te,

stringente fra le dita, premente sulle tue labbra
un ramoscello di menta selvaggia.

E il selvaggio profumo e il calor della mano
t'illanguidivano in una torbida sofferenza
di godimento;

e, boccheggiante, a poco a poco morivi,
pensando: "Ma il volto, il suo volto dov'è?"

Così ti svegliasti: cieca: nel fondo d'un livido
lago

chiuso per sempre su te col silenzio delle sue
acque.

🌿   (Dreams)

The Hand

You woke up before dawn, panting
  and shivering, because you had dreamed
  of your dead man.

You dreamed of him as he was in life, though
  cloaked in an intangible mantle of darkness.

You didn't see him, you felt him: you felt his
  large hand over you,

a sprig of wild mint tight between his fingers
  pressed against your lips.

And the wild fragrance and the warmth of that hand
  enfeebled you into a turbid aching
  pleasure;

and little by little in gasps you were dying,
  thinking: "But the face, where is his face?"

So you awoke: blind: at the bottom of a bruise-colored
  lake

enclosing you forever in the silence of its
  waters.

〰️   (I SOGNI)

Lo sguardo

*Solo il suo sguardo, questa notte, nel sogno
ti ritornò.*

*Non il corpo e non la voce e nemmeno
l'azzurra trasparenza degli occhi:*

*nulla fuor che lo sguardo, l'essenza dello
sguardo, la penetrante fissità dello sguardo.*

*Diceva la vita troncata e le trascorse dolcezze
e la malinconia della solitudine eterna;*

*e ti toglieva il respiro e s'affondava nelle
tue viscere, come un giorno l'amplesso vivente.*

*Senza palpebra e senza pupilla, fisso e caldo
nell'ombra, sguardo dell'invisibile amore!*

*Tu sapevi, ahimè! di sognarlo: sapevi che
l'alba dal pallido viso sarebbe venuta fra
breve a dissiparne l'incanto;*

*e le tue lagrime appassionate gocciavan nel
sonno sovra il guanciale in silenzio.*

※ (DREAMS)

The Look

Only his look returned to you tonight,
  in a dream.

Not the body and not the voice, not even
  the blue transparence of his eyes:

nothing but the look, the essence of the look,
  the penetrating fixity of the look.

It spoke of a life cut short, the sweetness of the past,
  and the melancholy of never-ending solitude;

it stole away your breath and plunged deep
  inside you, as in the days of his living embrace.

Without eyelids and without pupils, fixed and hot
  in the darkness, the gaze of invisible love!

You knew, alas! That you were dreaming of him: you knew
  that dawn with its pale face would soon come
  to dispel the enchantment;

and your impassioned tears kept falling in your
  sleep onto the pillow in silence.

☙   *(I sogni)*

Dialogo

"Con quale chiave apristi stanotte, o amato,
la piccola porta di strada?"

"Striscia ogni porta da sola sui cardini,
senza rumore, s'io venga o s'io vada."

"Venisti dunque con suole di feltro, ch'io
non t'intesi salire le scale?"

"Senza peso e senz'orma è il mio passo; ma
il cuore è di piombo nel petto, e fa male."

"Perché t'addossi rigido al muro, pendule ai
fianchi le braccia inerti?"

"Di qui non posso più oltre avanzare, non
son venuto che per vederti."

"Ma dammi un bacio, ma vedi che ho sete,
che muoio di sete della tua bocca!"

"Non ho più labbra se pur le scorgi, nell'aria
m'anniento se mano mi tocca."

"Ma nel tuo nulla perché non m'inghiotti?
Ma non hai dunque un po' di pietà?"

"Ancor patire, ancor pregare, ancora
attendere: l'ora verrà."

(DREAMS)

Dialogue

"With what key, o beloved, did you open
   the small door by the street tonight?"

"Each door glides on its own hinges, without
   noise, whether I come or go."

"Did you, then, come on soles of felt that I did not
   hear you climbing the stairs?"

"My step is without weight and without trace; though
   my heart is lead in my chest, and it aches."

"Why do you lean rigid against the wall, your arms
   inert, hanging, at your sides?"

"I can go no further than this, I've come only
   to see you."

"Just give me a kiss; you see that I thirst,
   that I die of thirst for your mouth!"

"I no longer have lips, though you see them,
   I would turn to nothing but air if a hand were to touch me."

"So, why don't you swallow me up in your nothing?
   Have you no pity, then?"

"There's more to endure, more to pray for, more
   to wait for: the hour will come."

La terra

Prona io mi distesi allargando le braccia,
tutta aderendo con il corpo alla terra,

e appoggiai l'orecchio alla terra, per sentir
l'erba crescere pian piano.

Non sentii crescere l'erba; ma dalle viscere
nere m'entrò nell'orecchio un rombo segreto:

che a traverso l'orecchio invase i miei sensi,
invase il mio cuore, lo dilatò, lo sommerse
nelle più cieche profondità.

E nella voce del mistero terrestre io riconobbi
la tua, o perduto, o ritrovato.

Perché tu eri divenuto la terra, e le tue vene
si diffondevano in tutte le fresche germinazioni.

E con tentacoli di radici e murmuri di polle
nascoste e fremiti lunghi di semi, o perduto,
o ritrovato, mi riprendesti con te.

The Earth

I lay prone, extending my arms, every part
  of my body adhering to the earth,

and I leaned my ear against the earth to hear
  the grass grow little by little.

I did not hear the grass grow, but from its black
  bowels a secret rumble entered my ear:

through my ear it invaded my senses,
  invaded my heart, dilated it, submerged it
  into the blindest depths.

And in the voice of terrestrial mystery I recognized
  yours, o lost one, o found one.

Because you had become the earth, and your veins
  were diffused in every budding sprout.

And with tentacles of roots, murmurs
  of hidden pools and long quivers of seeds,
  o lost one, o found one, you took me back with you.

La lampada d'oro

*Io fui dinanzi a te, mia vita, mia morte, la
lampada d'oro*

*in un angolo oscuro del tempio accesa dinanzi
all'immagine sacra.*

*Con umiltà divota trema la pia fiammella
fra nebbie d'incenso e palpiti di preghiere;*

*e quando par che vacilli, un'invisibile mano
aggiunge l'olio nel vaso.*

*Fu tolta l'immagine sacra, nudata al suo posto
la crosta grigiastra del muro:*

*non guarda il muro e non ode; ma innanzi
a lui cieco e sordo sempre arde nell'ombra
la lampada.*

*Veglia essa in fede, attendendo che tu ritorni
al suo fervore, o sposo:*

*e quando par che si spenga, l'amore alimenta
in silenzio la fiamma.*

The Golden Lamp

Here before you, my life, my death, I am
   the golden lamp,

lit in a dark corner of the temple, facing
   your sacred image.

With devout humility its small flame trembles
   amid fogs of incense and throbs of prayers;

and when it seems to flicker, an invisible hand
   adds oil to the vase.

Your sacred image was removed, exposing
   in its place the gray crust of the wall:

the wall neither sees nor hears; but before
   it, blind and deaf, the lamp always burns
   in the dark.

It keeps vigil in faith, waiting for you to return
   to its fervor, o bridegroom:

and when it seems to extinguish, love feeds
   its flame in silence.

ADA NEGRI

Rendimento di grazie

Al tuo piede che mosse, sicuro e diritto,
nell'ora giusta, verso di me:

alla tua mano che venne a calcarsi, nell'ora
giusta, sulla mia spalla, e l'impronta restò
nelle carni:

ai tuoi occhi che bella mi videro, giovine
e bella fra tutte le donne, e il mio viso
restò nella rètina:

alle tue labbra che tutta mi bevvero, e ogni
bacio mi uccise e da ognuno rinacqui:

al tuo cuore che in sé mi nascose, e nulla io
più seppi se non il suo palpito:

grazie sien rese in ogni ora del tempo, pel
corpo, per l'anima, per l'eternità.

E grazie sien rese in ogni ora del tempo
anche alla tua crudelissima morte,

che ti fece per me più alto e più fisso dei
monti, più chiaro e più fisso degli astri:

che t'inchiodò nel ricordo per me, per me
sola, disperatamente per me.

Giving Thanks

To your feet that moved, sure and direct,
   at the right time, toward me:

to your hand that came, at the right time, to press
   on my shoulder, and its imprint remained
   on my flesh:

to your eyes that saw me as beautiful, young
   and beautiful among all women, and my face
   remained in your retina:

to your lips that drank in all of me, and each
   kiss killed me and from each I was reborn:

to your heart that hid me inside it, and I knew
   nothing else but its beat:

may thanks be given at every hour
   for the body, for the soul, for eternity.

And may thanks be given at every hour
   also to your most cruel death,

that for me made you taller and more fixed
   than the mountains, brighter and more fixed than the stars:

that nailed you in memory for me, for me
   alone, desperately for me.

Ada Negri

Il colloquio

Quando ti avrò raggiunto sulla sponda del
 fiume di luce

e tu mi chiederai che ho fatto tant'anni senza
 di te,

io ti risponderò: "Ho continuato il colloquio."

Tu riderai per dolcezza tutto il riso de' tuoi
 bianchi denti,

e cingerai le mie spalle col tuo gesto securo
 di despota.

E lungo i prati di viole che fioriscono solo
 pei morti

continueremo il colloquio.

The Conversation

When I will have joined you on the bank
  of the river of light

and you will ask me what I have done these many years
  without you,

I will answer: "I have carried on the conversation."

Sweetly, you will laugh the full laughter
  of your white teeth,

and you will encircle my shoulders in the
  confident manner of a despot.

And along meadows of violets that bloom only
  for the dead

we shall continue the conversation.

Quies

Calmo pallore di luna sui bastioni ove fummo
felici negli abbacinanti meriggi,

o amato: e allora il sole senza tramonto ci
parve, senza agonia l'estate.

Freddo pallore di luna con ombre oblique
d'un nero azzurrigno d'inchiostro,

con alberi spogli scolpiti ciascuno in un gesto
di spasimo.

O amato, ove sei ora? E quale mare senza
riva inghiotte i pianti della mia disperazione?

Dopo sì lungo soffrire, "pace" implora il
sereno pallor della luna:

pace al cuore ancora vivente, pace al cuore
che non batte più.

Quies

The moon is calm and pale on the bastions where
  we were happy in the blinding mid-days,

o beloved: then, to us the sun seemed without setting,
  without anguish the summer.

The moon is cold and pale with slanting shadows,
  ink-black tinged in blue,

amid naked trees, each one carved in convulsive
  strokes.

O beloved, where are you now? And which sea
  without shore swallows up the tears of my despair?

After long suffering, "peace" entreats
  the serene pallor of the moon:

peace to the heart still living, peace to the heart
  that beats no more.

Il passante

*L'ignoto che passa e ti trova ancor degna
d'una fuggevole parola di desiderio,*

*forse perché nell'ombra della sera sì dolce di
maggio,*

*ancor ti splendono gli occhi, ancora ha vent'anni
la snella figura guizzante,*

*non sa che fosti amata, da colui che amasti
amata, in piena e superba letizia di amore,*

*e non hai membro e non lembo di carne e
non atomo d'anima che non rechi un segno di amore.*

*Che tu vivesti soltanto per amare colui che
t'amava,*

*e neppur se volessi potresti strappare da te
questa veste intessuta di amore.*

*Egli, ignaro, in te non più bella, in te non più
giovine, saluta la grazia del dio:*

*respira, passando, in te non più bella, in te
non più giovine, l'aroma prezioso del dio:*

*sol perché in te lo porti, reliquia dolce
all'ombra d'un sacrario.*

The Passer-By

The stranger passing by who finds you still worthy
   of a fleeting word of desire

— maybe because in the gentle shade of a May
   evening

your eyes still sparkle, your slim darting figure
   still looks twenty years old—

doesn't know that you were loved, loved by the one
   you loved, in the full and proud gladness of love,

and you have no limb, no speck of flesh,
   no atom of soul that doesn't bear a trace of love.

That you lived only to love him,
   who loved you,

and not even if you wanted could you strip away
   this garment interwoven with love.

Unaware, he greets the grace of god in you no longer
   beautiful, in you no longer young:

in passing, he breathes the precious aroma of god
   in you no longer beautiful, in you no longer young:

so you may carry it inside you, like a sweet relic
   in the shade of a shrine.

La rinunzia

Taci, fatti piccola piccola, avvolgi di veli
  il tuo viso,

vattene e non guardare il geranio sulla finestra,
  il convolvolo al cancello.

Chiudi i sensi al calore del sole che chiama
  a fiore delle vene il sangue,

chiudi il cuore al respiro dei campi che
  maturan la messe come grembo il figlio.

E se a uno svolto di siepe t'incontri a viso
  a viso con una coppia d'amanti

pallidi e lenti per felicità, e raccolti un nell'altro
  come in confessione,

balza all'indietro, càcciati nel primo folto
  di spini che ti nasconda,

sparisci dentro la terra per non vederli, per
  non ricordare

che ancor ieri tu fosti una donna, e annegavi
  ridendo e piangendo nell'amplesso del tuo
  uomo.

Renunciation

Hush, become ever so small, shroud
  your face with veils,

go away and don't look at the geranium
  on the window, the bindweed at the gate.

Shut your senses to the warmth of the sun that calls
  to surface the blood in your veins,

shut your heart to the breath of the fields
  that ripen the crop as the womb does a child.

And if at the bend of a hedgerow you encounter face
  to face a couple of lovers

pale and slow with happiness, engrossed
  in each other as if in confession,

jump backwards, steal into the first thicket
  of thorns that can hide you,

vanish inside the earth not to see them, not to
  remember

that only yesterday you were a woman, and you drowned
  laughing and crying in the embrace of your
  man.

Senza addio

Creatura, tutto da te fu udito: nulla più ti
rimane da ascoltare.

Tutto da te fu sofferto in patire e in gioire:
nulla più resta per le tue lagrime e pel tuo
riso.

Diléguati senza dire addio, con passo che non
tocchi terra, non guardando, dietro le palpebre
chiuse, che i tuoi ricordi dentro di te:

nessuno si avvedrà del tuo sparire, e tu non
farai partendo più rumore dell'ombra di
un'ala di rondine.

Vi fu dunque un tempo nel quale il tuo cuore
tremò di delizia mirando le rose sbocciare
nel sole,

e, come le rose al sole, si aperse all'uomo in
tutto lo splendore e l'ardore del sangue?

Creatura, calato è il velo, spento il desiderio,
rotto il legame fra la tua vita e l'umanità:

cerca il cancello ch'è in fondo alla strada, non
hai che da spingere: la taciturna che veglia
unge d'olio ogni notte i suoi cardini.

Without Goodbye

Child, you have heard everything: there is nothing
   left for you to listen to.

You have endured everything of suffering and of rejoicing:
   nothing remains for your tears and your
   laughter.

Vanish without saying goodbye, with footsteps
   not touching the ground, not looking behind your
   closed eyelids at anything but the memories inside:

no one will notice your disappearance, and your
   leaving will make no more noise than the shadow
   of a swallow's wing.

Was there ever a time your heart
   shook with delight admiring roses bloom
   in the sun,

and, like roses to the sun, it opened up to a man
   in the full splendor and heat of blood?

Child, the veil has dropped, desire is spent,
   the link between your life and humanity, broken:

look for the gate at the end of the road, you have
   only to push: the taciturn woman on watch
   oils its hinges each night.

Nei giardini del silenzio

Nei giardini del silenzio
ove stai, calmo e solo, in disparte,
una notte io ti porterò
questa mia povera anima fedele
che non può vivere
se non nell'ombra della tua ombra.

Gigante sarà la tua ombra,
ma sì dolci, sì teneri gli occhi.
Non oserò dirti parola.
Non oserò chiederti, o mio
amato, perché sei scomparso
così, senza dirmi addio.

Me ne starò tutta quieta
ed umile, ai tuoi ginocchi.
Oh, pur che tu non mi mandi
via, pur che tu le tue grandi
mani m'imponga sul capo,
in pace, per l'eternità!

Tratterrò in gola il respiro
per non turbarti. Io sola
accanto a te solo: su noi
un palpito azzurro di stelle,
e il vuoto, e l'assenza del tempo:

forse, la verità.

In the Gardens of Silence

In the gardens of silence
  where you are, calm and alone, apart,
  I shall deliver to you one night
  my poor faithful soul
  that cannot live
  unless in the shadow of your shadow.

Gigantic will be your shadow,
  but so sweet, so tender your eyes.
  I won't dare say a word.
  I won't dare ask you, my
  beloved, why you disappeared
  like that, without saying goodbye.

I will stay quiet
  and humble, at your knees.
  Oh, if only you won't send me
  away, if only you'll lay your great
  hands on my head,
  in peace, for eternity!

I will hold my breath in my throat
  not to disturb you. I alone
  beside you alone: above us
  a blue pulsing of stars,
  and the void, and the absence of time:

perhaps, the truth.

ADA NEGRI

Via della Passione

Via della Passione
breve diritta deserta
chiusa in fondo dal tempio che splende
nel rossoviolaceo
fulgor del sole a tramonto.
Tramonto di marzo
con sentor di vïole nell'aria.
Bianco l'asfalto ed arido,
tra file di case
senza sguardo. Non passa nessuno.
Cielo sereno che smuore,
tempio che arde che arde.

Via della Passione,
ecco la tua sorella
di carne
al par di te deserta
nel tramonto senza speranza.
Somiglia il tuo tempio al mio cuore
che arde in solitudine
e nulla attende in premio dell'ardore.
Ritorna la primavera:
venuta è con l'aspro vento,
ha pieno di gemmule il grembo,
non per me, non per te!
Noi taciturne vegliamo
il sogno che non vuol morire,
mentre gli uomini vanno per altre
strade, ed il cielo lontano
non vede, e la terra non sente.

Quando la notte sarà caduta
io m'accovaccerò rasente il muro,
come una cagna sperduta;
e l'ombra senza nome
confonderà la mia
la tua malinconia,
via della Passione.

Way of the Passion

Way of the Passion
  short straight deserted
  closed at the end by a temple that shines
  in the purple-red
  brightness of the setting sun.
  March sunset
  with a scent of violets in the air.
  Dry, white asphalt
  between rows of houses
  without view. No one goes by.
  The serene sky grows pale,
  the temple burns and burns.

Way of the Passion,
  here is your sister
  of flesh
  deserted like you
  without hope in the sunset.
  Your temple resembles my heart
  that burns in solitude
  awaiting no prize for its passion.
  Spring returns:
  it has come with a harsh wind,
  her womb filled with buds,
  not for me, not for you!
  In silence, we watch over
  the dream that won't die,
  while men go down other
  roads, and the faraway sky
  doesn't see, and the earth doesn't hear.

When night comes,
  I will crouch against the wall,
  like a she-dog astray;
  and the nameless shadow
  will blur mine
  your melancholy,
  way of the Passion.

ADA NEGRI

Ode canicolare

O mio geloso bene,
  torrida nel ricordo,
  canicolare estate
  ch'io vissi errando
  trasfusa in gioia
  nel tuo biancore accecante,
  nelle tue nozze orgiastiche
  del calor con la luce,
  nelle tue notti stellate
  accese di rapidi lampi!

Trascorsa e pure eterna,
  unica nella mia vita,
  per me fiorita
  dai cementi nervati di ferro,
  dai colmigni fumanti nell'afa,
  dagli asfalti bollenti in odore
  di catrame, dai platani bronzei
  boccheggianti d'asfissia all'azzurro,
  nella
  città che mi vide bella!

Incandescenza
  immobile dei marciapiedi
  e di case altissime in fila.
  Cielo di piombo liquefatto,
  persiane chiuse
  celanti il languore
  di femmine seminude
  distese sui letti in sudore.
  Botteghe oscure
  e mute, odoranti di spezie,
  lattee risa di cocco ghiacciato
  su glauche lastre di zinco,
  macchie gialle sulfuree verdicce

Summer Ode

O my beloved season,
  torrid in memory
  are the dog days
  I spent wandering
  transfused in joy
  in your blinding whiteness,
  your lustful nuptials
  of heat with light,
  your star-filled nights
  lit with flashes of lightning!

Past yet eternal,
  unequaled in my life,
  you bloomed for me
  from cement works veined with iron,
  from smoking roof-vents in the humid heat,
  from boiling asphalt smelling
  of tar, from bronze sycamores
  gasping for air toward the sky,
  in the
  city that saw me beautiful!

Immobile
  incandescence of sidewalks
  and tall houses in a row.
  Sky of molten lead,
  shutters closed
  concealing the languor
  of women lying half-naked
  in sweat on their beds.
  Shops dark
  and silent, fragrant with spices,
  milky smiles of chilled coconut
  on blue-gray slabs of zinc,
  stains yellow sulfuric greenish

di frutti e d'ortaggi
ammonticchiati nei fóndachi,
fontanelle nei crocicchi,
giardini vuoti,
angoli di freschezza
sì radi, sì dolci, nell'urbe
offerta al sole,
penetrata ammalata di sole.

Di voi m'intrisi
e godetti nel profondo,
acri fermenti
di cose e d'uomini,
insanità
terribile della città,
sete dei tetti e dei lastrici,
ridde di polvere a vortici.
Tanta luce saziò i miei occhi
che abbacinati rimasero
forse per sempre.
Da tal vampa il mio cuor fu combusto
che incenerito rimase
forse per sempre.
E tu, che hai nome dall'aria,
datore di forza e di gioia,
tu solo a me sola,
comparso scomparso
con le prime rose del maggio,
coi primi grappoli dell'ottobre!

Ci amammo
nella città felice,
da lei posseduti
e liberi in essa, padroni
delle sue piazze uguali
ad affocati deserti,
de' tortuosi suoi vicoli

of fruits and vegetables
heaped up in crates,
drinking fountains at crossroads,
empty gardens,
corners of freshness
so rare, so sweet, in the city
given up to the sun,
penetrated ailing with sun.

Immersed in you,
  I took pleasure in your depth,
  the acrid ferment
  of things and of men,
  the dread
  insanity of the city,
  thirsting rooftops and pavements,
  turmoil of dust and whirls.
  So much light filled my eyes
  that they remained dazzled
  maybe forever.
  Such flame burned my heart
  reducing it to ashes
  maybe forever.
  And you, named by the air,
  giver of strength and joy,
  you alone to me alone,
  appeared, disappeared
  with the first roses of May,
  the first grapes of October!

We loved one another
  in the happy city,
  by her possessed
  and free in her, lords
  of her squares that were
  smoldering deserts,
  of her winding alleys

pieni di baci e d'oblìo,
de' suoi fosforescenti
notturni silenzi, che parvero
unire il cielo alla terra
nell'azzurro di due firmamenti.
Ci amammo
come tu fossi l'uomo
primo, io la donna
prima, nell'alba del mondo.
Nulla fu innanzi l'amore,
non tempo, non opra, non legge:
nulla fu dopo l'amore,
fuor che il ricordo.

…O vita,
s'io debba a lungo
esserti schiava, se ottundere
a poco a poco tu debba
le forze per cui mi donasti
me stessa, — o vita, —
non togliermi la memoria.
Ch'io dentro di me fino all'ultimo
serbi la visione
e il senso della stagione
senz'ombra e senza sonno,
specchio fedele alla mia
felicità d'esser donna:
connubio di due violenze,
il mio gioire, il suo ardere.
Dolce mi sia l'esser viva
se pur non più giovine, solo
per riconoscermi,
per ritrovare
nello splendor del ricordo
la mia sostanza solare.

filled with kisses and oblivion,
phosphorescent
night silences, seeming
to join the sky to the earth
in the blue of two firmaments.
We loved one another
as if you were the first
man, I the first
woman, in the dawn of the world.
Nothing came before love,
not time, not work, not law:
nothing came after love,
except for its memory.

       …O life,
if I must be your slave
for long, if you must blunt
bit by bit
the strengths by which you gave me
Self — o life —
do not steal away my memory
so I may keep to the end
the vision
and the feel of this season
without shade and without sleep,
true mirror of my
happiness in being a woman:
the union of two forces,
my rejoicing, its ardor.
Sweet may it be to live,
though no longer young, if only
to recognize,
to find again
in the splendor of remembrance
my essence of sun.

Notturno della luna

Notte, divina notte,
non so chi chiami, non so chi pianga,
se i grilli o le roride erbe,
se l'anima mia
o l'anima dell'infinito.

Notte, divina notte,
ancor tutta intrisa di lagrime
per la recente pioggia
e così grave di aromi
che la mia carne n'è inferma,
dietro ombre di nubi la luna
cammina cammina cercando
la strada che non troverà,
la strada della felicità.

Notte, divina notte,
dimmi ove è nascosto il mio amore:
ch'era mio e le mie braccia
non bastarono a custodirlo,
ch'era mio ed io ero sua
e adesso non ho più nulla
e non sono più di nessuno.
Conducimi passo per passo
lungo le vie della luna
fin ch'io lo tocchi senza vederlo,
fin ch'io lo stringa senza baciarlo,
poi che non ha più bocca:
e in esso affondi, siccome
dentro la fossa una morta,

e sia silenzio.

Nocturne

Night, divine night,
  I don't know who's calling; I don't know who's crying,
  whether the crickets or the moist grasses,
  whether my soul
  or the soul of the infinite.

Night, divine night,
  still drenched with tears
  from the recent rain
  and so fraught with aromas
  that sicken my flesh,
  behind shadows of clouds the moon
  travels, travels in search of
  the road it will not find,
  the road of happiness.

Night, divine night,
  tell me where my beloved is hidden:
  he who was mine and my arms
  were not enough to protect him,
  who was mine and I was his
  and now I have nothing
  and I belong to no one.
  Lead me step by step
  along the paths of the moon
  till I may touch him without seeing him,
  till I may hold him without kissing him,
  since he no longer has lips:
  and may I sink into him, as
  a dead woman inside a grave,

  and may there be silence.

PACE

Per tutti i pianti ch'io piansi, grazia dei martiri,
senso di pace, discendi in me:

spoglia ormai d'ogni bene del mondo, placata
e in ginocchio ti ricevo dal cielo.

L'anima chiara si schiude ad accoglierti, e
nulla è più in essa che di te non sia degno.

O dono di serenità, così sulle mani talvolta
mi caddero i fiori del mandorlo, nei
ventosi mattini di marzo.

O dono di carità, ma tu, se candido come
un fiore, sei forte come la morte.

O dono di morte, confessa io sono e comunicata:
l'anima è pronta per partire con
te senza ritorno.

Peace

For all the tears I cried, grace of the martyrs,
  feeling of peace, descend upon me:

by now stripped of every good of the world, calmed
  and on my knees, I receive you from heaven.

My clear soul unfolds to welcome you, and it
  has nothing left that is unworthy of you.

O gift of serenity, like this blossoms fell
  from the almond tree onto my hands at times,
  on windy mornings in March.

O gift of charity, though white as a flower,
  you are strong as death.

O gift of death, I have made my confession and received
  my communion: my soul is ready to leave with you
  without returning.

Voto

*Non segua io nel mondo altra legge se non
quella dei fiori e degli astri,*

or che in pace il tuo spirito è in me.

*La mia voce non entri nei cuori che coi limpidi
accenti di Dio,*

or che in pace il tuo spirito è in me.

*Le mie mani sien colme di rose per giuncarne
le strade dell'ombra,*

or che in pace il tuo spirito è in me.

*Ogni pensiero sia opra ed ogni germe sia
frutto ed ogni pianto sia canto,*

or che in pace il tuo spirito è in me.

Vow

May I follow no law in the world if not
  that of the flowers and of the stars,

now that in peace your spirit is in me.

May my voice enter no hearts if not with the
  pure accents of God,

now that in peace your spirit is in me.

May my hands be filled with roses to strew them
  across roads of darkness,

now that in peace your spirit is in me.

May each thought become action and each seed
  become fruit and each cry become song,

now that in peace your spirit is in me.

Domani

Domani è aprile, e tu verrai per condurmi
incontro all'ultima primavera.

Donde verrai, come verrai, non so; ma senza
soffrire potrò rivederti.

Soave sarà nella tua la mia mano, soave il
mio passo al tuo fianco.

Occhi d'infanzia i nostri, a specchio innocente
del novo miracolo verde.

Andremo per orti e frutteti, a capo scoperto
nel sole, senza far male ai santi germogli.

In punta di piedi, per tema si stacchin dai
rami le rosee farfalle dei peschi,

e trepidi e senza respiro, per non turbar pur
con l'aria i fiori dell'ultimo sogno.

E di quello che fu della carne, nulla verrà
ricordato.

E di quello che fu del dolore, nulla verrà
ricordato.

E di quel che è della vita eterna farà pieno di
canti il silenzio.

Non io tua, non tu mio: dello spazio: radendo
la terra con ali invisibili,

sempre più lievi nell'aria, sempre più immersi
nel cielo,

fino a quando la notte ci assuma ai suoi vasti
sepolcri di stelle.

Tomorrow

Tomorrow is April, and you will come to guide me
  toward the last spring.

From where you will come, how you will come, I don't know;
  but I will be able to see you again without suffering.

Gentle will be my hand in yours, gentle
  my step at your side.

Ours the eyes of childhood, innocent mirrors
  of the new green miracle.

We shall go through gardens and orchards, our heads bare
  in the sun, without harming the sacred buds.

On tiptoe, for fear the rose-colored butterflies of the peach
  trees might fall away from the branches,

anxious and without breathing, not to disturb even
  with air the flowers of the last dream.

And what was of flesh, nothing will be
  remembered.

And what was of sorrow, nothing will be
  remembered.

And what is of eternal life will fill
  the silence with song.

I not yours, you not mine: of space: grazing
  the earth with invisible wings,

ever lighter in air, ever more immersed
  in the sky,

till night shall assume us in its vast
  sepulchers of stars.

Ada Negri

FIRST LINE INDEX

ITALIAN

Sole di mezzogiorno, nel luglio felice	2
Egli ti amò. Non avesti altro bene. Umìliati	4
Confitta è alla croce e non la darebbe per	8
Entrasti improvviso, lasciando spalancata la	10
Venne in cerca di te	12
Quando tu le camminasti accanto con	14
Quando tu venisti, una notte, verso il suo	16
Quando il canto del gallo segò il cielo, ed	18
Quando il tuo corpo immoto fu tolto ai suoi	20
Brevi erano le tue lettere, precise, tutte muscolo	22
Ella anche ti amava nelle tue collere taciturne	24
O tardi venuto, nel tempo in cui la porta si chiude	26
La donna che or vive nascosta come una	28
Accetto la cosa tremenda, per seguire la tua	30
E tu che farai, anima, per renderti in vita	32
Oggi ti cerco e non ti trovo, non sei né in	34
Una foglia cadde del platano, un fruscio	36
Quando tu mi stringevi, divino carnefice,	38
Alto è il muro che fiancheggia la mia strada	40
Vanno per vie deserte tagliate a metà dalla	42
Gioia del giorno in cui egli t'addusse fra	44
Non chiamarmi, non dirmi nulla	46
Ti svegliasti avanti l'alba, in affanno ed	48
Solo il suo sguardo, questa notte, nel sogno	50
"Con quale chiave apristi stanotte, o amato	52
Prona io mi distesi allargando le braccia	54
Io fui dinanzi a te, mia vita, mia morte, la	56
Al tuo piede che mosse, sicuro e diritto	58
Quando ti avrò raggiunto sulla sponda del	60
Calmo pallore di luna sui bastioni ove fummo	62
L'ignoto che passa e ti trova ancor degna	64
Taci, fatti piccola piccola, avvolgi di veli	66
Creatura, tutto da te fu udito: nulla più ti	68
Nei giardini del silenzio	70
Via della Passione	72
O mio geloso bene	74
Notte, divina notte	80
Per tutti i pianti ch'io piansi, grazia dei martiri	82
Non segua io nel mondo altra legge se non	84
Domani è aprile, e tu verrai per condurmi	86

English

Noonday sun, that happy July	3
He loved you. You had no other love. Be humble	5
She is nailed to the cross and would not trade it	9
You came in suddenly, leaving	11
She came looking for you	13
you walked beside her with the pliant	15
When you came, one night, to her bed	17
When the crow of the rooster sawed the sky	19
When your motionless body was removed from her	21
Your letters were brief, precise, all muscle	23
She loved you also in your quiet rages	25
You came at the time the door closes	27
The woman who now lives hidden like a wounded	29
I accept this dreadfulness, in order to follow	31
And what will you do, soul, to become worthy	33
Today I search for you and do not find you; you're neither	35
A leaf fell from the sycamore, a rustle	37
Whenever you gripped me, wan and demented	39
High is the wall that flanks my road	41
They go down deserted roads cut in half	43
Joyful the day he brought you among	45
Don't call me, say nothing	47
You woke up before dawn, panting	49
Only his look returned to you tonight	51
"With what key, o beloved, did you open	53
I lay prone, extending my arms, every part	55
Here before you, my life, my death, I am	57
To your feet that moved, sure and direct	59
When I will have joined you on the bank	61
The moon is calm and pale on the bastions where	63
The stranger passing by who finds you still worthy	65
Hush, become ever so small, shroud	67
Child, you have heard everything: there is nothing	69
In the gardens of silence	71
Way of the Passion	73
O my beloved season	75
Night, divine night	81
For all the tears I cried, grace of the martyrs	83
May I follow no law in the world if not	85
Tomorrow is April, and you will come to guide me	87

*This Work Was Completed on December 1,
2010 at Italica Press, New York.
It Was Set in ITC Giovanni
& Printed on 55-lb.
Natural Paper.*

www.ingramcontent.com/pod-product-compliance
Lightning Source LLC
Chambersburg PA
CBHW031155160426
43193CB00008B/383